CALIFORNIA COLONIAL
THE SPANISH AND RANCHO REVIVAL STYLES

Elizabeth McMillian, Ph.D.

Schiffer Publishing Ltd

4880 Lower Valley Road, Atglen, PA 19310 USA

Photography by Matt Gainer and Elizabeth McMillian

Library of Congress Cataloging-in-Publication Data

McMillian, Elizabeth Jean.
California colonial: the Spanish and Rancho revival styles / Elizabeth McMillian ;
photography by Matt Gainer and Elizabeth McMillian.
p. cm.
ISBN: 0-7643-1460-2
1. Architecture, Domestic--California. 2. Architecture, Spanish colonial--Califor-
nia. 3. Ranch houses--California. 4. Architecture--California--20th century. I.
Gainer, Matt. II. Title.
NA7235.C22 M39 2001
728.3'7'09794--dc21
2001005112

Designed by Bonnie M. Hensley
Cover design by Bruce M. Waters
Type set in Geometric 231 Hv BT/Aldine 721 BT

ISBN: 0-7643-1460-2
Printed in China

Published by Schiffer Publishing Ltd.
4880 Lower Valley Road
Atglen, PA 19310
Phone: (610) 593-1777; Fax: (610) 593-2002
E-mail: Schifferbk@aol.com
Please visit our web site catalog at
www.schifferbooks.com

This book may be purchased from the publisher.
Include $3.95 for shipping. Please try your bookstore first.
We are always looking for people to write books on new and related subjects. If you
have an idea for a book please contact us at the above address.
You may write for a free catalog.

In Europe, Schiffer books are distributed by
Bushwood Books
6 Marksbury Avenue
Kew Gardens
Surrey TW9 4JF England
Phone: 44 (0) 20-8392-8585; Fax: 44 (0) 20-8392-9876
E-mail: Bushwd@aol.com
Free postage in the UK. Europe: air mail at cost.

CONTENTS

ACKNOWLEDGMENTS

I thank Peter and Nancy Schiffer for their patience and diligence in producing this work. Among homeowners and collectors who opened their homes to me, I thank Regina Drucker, Maxine Gray, Margie and Lawrence Schneider, Len Hill and Ann Daniel, Jon Cottrell, Rod and Gina Guerra, Neil Korpinen, and Corrine and Tony Shukartsi. The knowledgeable staffs of the house museums shown here are also much appreciated, including: the California Historical Society based in the Lummis House and tour guide Barry Ryan; the Will Rogers House and State Park, along with its former museum curator Nancy Mendez and Mike Allen; the Hearst Castle and its chief curator Hoyt Fields and staff Jeff Payne and Jim Allen; the Adamson House, its senior superintendent Hayden W. Sohm, and Lynette Falk; the Casa del Herrero, its former director Jean Smith Goodrich and collector-dealer Mike Haskell for his excellent information on its furnishings; the William S. Hart Historic House and Park, its administrator Zandra Stanley and Sheila Fernandez, and finally, the Antelope Valley Indian Museum and its curator Edra Moore.

My gratitude is extended to many others who contributed information and contacts, including State Parks curator Susan Doniger, landscape architect Karen Adams, Hearst Castle scholar Taylor Coffman, editor Melissa Brandzel, tile collector Christi Walden, actor/collector Kevin West; Catalina Island ceramic artist Will Richards; Santa Barbara architects Robert Easton, Henry Lenny and Tom Bollay, tile scholar Joseph Taylor and the Tile Heritage Foundation, collector/antiques dealer Don Shorts, and writers/regional historians Leslie Heumann and Diane Kanner.

This book would not have been possible except for the assistance of photographer/artist Matt Gainer and the generous contribution of the resources section from interior designer Bettye Young.

I've been told by architect Ricardo Legorreta that in Mexico, they call a Spanish or Mexican-style house in California, a "casa California" since it is neither truly Spanish nor Mexican. Whether accurate or not, many of these houses successfully reproduce the tactile quality of the materials and architectural forms of the movement that many still find the inspiring bases of traditional Mexican architecture. The Spanish style also remains the touchstone and the essence of Mexico's contemporary work, such as Legorreta's.

California's style had its roots in Mexico through the Spanish Franciscans, their Mexican universities and the eighteenth century styles that Mexico derived from Spain. The following study presents the historical differences between the *Plateresco*, *Churrigueresco* and *Desornamentado* styles and reveals the rich and complex culture that inspires the casa California. *Mudéjar* treatment of details and the influence of vernacular works from Andalusia also illuminate the California development. We recognize that key historic Spanish monuments inspired both the Mexican and California revivals and they continue to provide a framework of architectural details and furnishings. They have influenced elements of a number of Southern California Spanish style monuments, such as Hearst Castle at San Simeon, the Adamson House in Malibu and Casa del Herrero in Montecito.

The Spanish style is as alive today as classicism, and the American adoption of the Spanish-Mexican style includes the classical form through the robust interpretation of the Hispanic culture with the decorative imprint of Arabic craftsmanship. In Southern California, there is the same zest for life expressed in a love for color, tile surfaces, carved wood, sculpted stucco and stone, and intricate metalworking. Also, the California climate fosters the Spanish manner of indoor-outdoor living, landscaping with water works and lush planting.

In the early decades of this century, the Spanish period style in America was an elitist one although primarily based on common vernacular forms, and in California, it represented the coming of age and prominence of the state and its inhabitants. Today, both the Spanish Mission Era and the Mexican Hacienda Era are important to their contemporary revival. While numbers of aficionados, collectors and connoisseurs recognize the cultural inheritance of the region, modern designers and architects have abstracted and developed the style. They frequently abandon the images and axial approaches of the 1920s but they find the many Spanish concepts, decorative details and furnishings useful to their understanding and practical for their design approach. Imagery, motifs and materials from *any* of the Spanish periods may be reassembled for today's life style and amenities.

It is an important observation that the California ranch house style derives from the Hispanic colonial hacienda built on the ranchos in the region. During the 1920s and 1930s, the ranch house was fictionalized to a great extent by Western movies and the cowboy stars who built a number of them. Anglo farmhouse aspects were added and many appear purely an American vernacular style. However, in its straightforward honesty, the California ranch house theoretically represents a form of folk architecture because it derives from its Spanish-Mexican colonial roots and reflects the assimilation into the region's culture. The rancho hacienda, or ranch house, is quite appropriately another version of the Spanish-Mexican tradition and truly another form of casa California.

Mexico's long Spanish colonial history is also found throughout Southern California in modern versions, such as Ricardo Legorreta's 1990-91 Shapiro Residence, located in a Los Angeles suburb and now well maintained by present owners Corrine and Anthony Shukartsi. Legoretta explains his abstract geometric forms are based on "the zocalos, plazas, churches, colonial haciendas, the

the missions.

The first *santos* were made by the friars or under their direction, but eventually itinerant craftsmen, called *santeros*, executed these commissions for the local mission, church, or domestic chapel. Images of the saints painted on wood panels were called *retablos*. Other paintings on buffalo or elk hide are now extremely rare.

Sculpted figures were called *bultos* and were carved of wood, covered with gesso and painted bright colors. Many *bultos* were dressed in elaborate vestments like those made in, and brought from, Mexico.

In late nineteenth century California, the work of the *santeros* fell out of fashion and was replaced with plaster statues and prints from church-good suppliers. Altar screens were painted over or trimmed with imitation Gothic detail. By the twentieth century, the *santeros* only had a few commissions for *bultos* and *santos* for family chapels. A few *santeros* still practice in the Southwest, and currently there's a renewed interest in the craft.

PART TWO
MEXICAN COLONIAL HACIENDA ERA, 1821-1849

Simple vernacular hacienda and rancho structures began to be built shortly after the Spanish missions and *presidios* of the Mission Era. Plain domestic structures were built by Spanish, Mexican and Anglo settlers, and became more abundant after 1821 when Mexico became independent from Spain and took over its colonial outpost. Alta California then entered what has been called the Hacienda, or Rancho, Era of colonization.

This phase and its Mexican government were brief and chaotic. In 1834, the governor of California and Mexico City officials secularized the missions and took mission property, cattle and grain. When it was clear that Anglos were taking over the region and California would soon be an American state, provincial Mexican governors sold and handed out land grants to friends and relatives. During the twenty-eight year Mexican takeover, over five hundred grants were dispensed compared to the twenty to twenty-five large land grants of the earlier fifty-two year Spanish Era.

California towns and scattered ranchos grew and expanded while Anglo pioneers impinged on Spanish, Mexican and Native American property. Only a few decades earlier, Spanish settlers were the army officers, rancho owners and government officials, controlling the *presidios*, ranches and towns. The Spanish settlers became known as "Californios," a term for landowning settlers, distinguishing them from lower-class, landless "Mexicanos." Class strife between *Californios* and *Mexicanos* further disenfranchised the Native Americans.

After the 1821 Mexican takeover of California and the 1834 secularization of the missions, there was a subsequent increase in the number of *Mexicanos*, and, after the 1849 gold rush in northern Alta California, large numbers of Mexican opportunists came up from the Sonora province. The last years of the brief Mexican colonization were a Wild West period of *vaqueros* and cowboys. A few cattle rustling and mine looting incidents served to galvanize the upper-class *Californios* with the *Mexicanos* — both classes together considered as *Mexicanos* battling against encroaching Anglos. From 1846 through 1848, the United States fought Mexico over Alta California. The battle was settled with the Treaty of Guadaloupe-Hidalgo and the United States' purchase of California. By 1850, the region was made a state, and Monterey was established as its capital.

ADOBES: HACIENDA AND RANCHO VERNACULAR STYLES

The earliest California adobes — the casas in the pueblos and the haciendas on the ranchos or mission properties — differed little from those in New Mexico, but they developed from the old Mexican-type structure of conical thatch- or gable-roofed adobe *jacals*. The thick mud-brick walls were appropriate for the climate. Most were one-story houses with few rooms, without hallways. When the roofs were flat, they were made from a type of asphalt mixed with coarse sand and fastened all around with narrow boards cut through with small drains. Pitched roofs were covered with hollow tile. The better houses had pitched roofs that were with large tiles. The haciendas had wide verandahs, also called *portales*, supported by wooden posts. They usually had bare clay floors; later houses had wood floors. Often, vernacular adobe buildings were left in their natural adobe color and their walls were two to three feet of adobe brick, with each square brick approximately 18 inches long.

A fine example of the hacienda would be the Casa de Estudillo in San Diego. It was built in 1827 by a *Californio*, Jose Antonio Estudillo, son of the Spanish Captain of the Royal Presidio of San Diego. Estudillo held many public offices and also had large land holdings. His adobe hacienda was a typical U-shaped plan forming a courtyard with four quadrants and a central fountain. The twelve-room adobe had five-foot-thick walls, a tile roof over heavy timbers and plank floors. It is a fine vernacular example of the courtyard adobe hacienda, as would be built on a successful rancho, and its great hall also served as the town chapel.

Corredors follow the Estudillo U-plan and surround the courtyard garden laid out in its original form with four quadrants and a central circular fountain. With few exceptions, the twelve rooms of the adobe were reached only through doors from the exterior hallway.

The Estudillos, one of the founding families of the *presidio* of San Diego, began a large U-planned adobe hacienda in 1827. Restored and used as a public museum, its plain exterior and long, low appearance provide an excellent image of the typical California adobe. Well-defined lintels cap the few windows and doors that open the five-foot thick, white-washed walls and heavy timbers support the low-angled tile roof. A belfry was added since the Estudillos' great hall also served as the town chapel.

A Unique Monterey Development

Monterey was a popular seaport town first settled by the Spanish during the colonization period, and later, in the 1830s to 1850s — the period spanning the Mexican takeover to U.S. statehood — a number of Mexicans came to try their luck at a better life at the successful port. Also, arriving by ship, a number of Anglo pioneers who were New England ship-builders settled here, bringing their woodworking and carpentry skills to the area.

Amidst the variety of settlers and social-political change, the port saw a unique architectural development. It was the mix of adobe construction and wood classical decoration and it demonstrated a form of cultural assimilation, using elements of traditional adobe casas and haciendas from the Spaniards and the Mexicans, along with elements of federal style buildings from the Anglo pioneers.

Monterey's adobe houses tended to be whitewashed and roofed with red tile or sometimes with wood-shingle. The many decorative wood details the ship carpenters gave to the houses provided their unique New England appearance. The carpenter-builders generally built two-story adobes that featured a lower wood porch, like a *portal*, and an upper wood balcony.

It was the upper wood balcony that became the trademark of the Monterey colonial house and its revival. However, many Monterey-style houses from the revival decades lacked true Monterey balconies, which generally fronted one or more facades, extending from one end of the building to the other and frequently had closed ends for privacy and weather control. The most common Monterey balcony was one with supporting posts from ground to roof, but occasionally there would be a rare cantilevered balcony and cantilevered roof without supporting posts.

Typical wood New England elements also included double-hung glazed windows; classical detailing to window and door surrounds; picket fences around the gardens; and louvered shutters — not the more common spindle- or plank-type shutters of the Spanish-Mexican tradition.

One of the best Monterey-style houses is the Larkin House, an adobe that has a balcony that runs around three sides of the structure, and moldings and balusters that reflect New England carpentry techniques.

Despite its delicate wood details, the Larkin House in Monterey, California, 1834-1835, is a two-story adobe structure. The house was built by a New Englander, Mr. T.O. Larkin, who was born in Massachusetts but spent ten years in North Carolina. Larkin's choice for a continuous upper balcony and lower porch may have derived from the Carolinas' tidewater dwellings, which, in fact, likely evolved from Caribbean prototypes.

The Larkin House has multi-paned, double-hung windows, multi-paneled doors and straight railing balusters that were typical of New England houses. The house is considered the first adobe to have an upper balcony, from which California's "Monterey style" arose. In addition, it is thought to be the first California house with glass windows and an interior fireplace.

During the next phase of California's history — a watershed period that began with the 1849-1850 U.S. purchase and statehood, and the discovery of gold in 1849 in the northern part of the state — the variety of settlers, social and political change continued. Thousands of Anglos and American citizens came from the north and eastern portions of the United States, bringing in their formal traditions and building methods, and many Asians came in to construct the railroads, joining with the Mexicans who came from the south in their common goal to seek their fortunes.

Unfortunately, the Anglo-American Land Act of 1851 and the complex system of taxation brought about the demise of the Mexican and Spanish rancheros — not to mention the Native Americans — all of whom could not confirm their land grant status, figure out and/or pay their taxes. From the 1850s to 1890s, many Spanish and Mexican rancheros lost their holdings to the Anglos, and they also lost their political power and their social status.

1860s to 1880s International Exoticism

In the late 1860s, a fascination with international cultures spread throughout most of the American states. The 1870s and 1880s also saw the rise of collections of European paintings, accounts of exotic travel and romantic tales set in Oriental and Moorish settings. At the same time in California, Anglos moved in and built wood and shingle Victorian houses with a plethora of bric-a-brac elements and delightful decorative styles. For these savvy settlers, adobes and rancho haciendas were historic but too simple and unattractive. If they chose a Spanish or Mexican style, they were much more interested in the exotic Spanish and Moorish details they saw in books rather than any decorative elements found at the Spanish mission structures. Most Victorian houses of this style have since been destroyed along with their cusped and keyhole arches, onion domes, and open circular kiosks, porches or towers.

One writer caught up in the spirit of foreign exoticism, looked closer to home for her subjects. In the early 1880s, Helen Hunt Jackson — originally from Boston — began to be interested in the treatment of the Native Americans and discovered that California could be explored for its native subjects as well as its pioneering Spaniards and Mexicans. She started writing about the demise of all three groups under United States statehood. Her articles from the early 1880s included "Father Junipero and His Work" and "The Condition of the Mission Indians." After the furor that her 1881 *A Century of Dishonor* created, President Chester Arthur appointed Hunt to a federal commission investigating the plight of the Native Americans on the California missions.

From 1881 to 1885, Jackson made three trips to California, which focused primarily on the southern portion of the state, and she gathered bits of information and tales about the mission natives. These trips gave her the material for *Glimpses of the*

Missions, 1883, with Henry Sandham's drawings of the structures in their ruined state, and for her novel *Ramona*, 1884. Jackson is particularly known for *Ramona*, a tragic love story between the half-Spanish *Californio* and half-Native American Ramona and a "noble savage" named Alessandro. It gave a romanticized picture of Old California undergoing traumatic ethnic changes and political shift to statehood.

To this day, *Ramona* provides an excellent picture of Southern California, its landscape and its various building types during its early statehood phase. While Jackson's missions were better covered in her non-fictional *Glimpses of the Missions*, in the novel, they are clearly tributes to the cultural power of the Spaniards, Mexicans and Native Americans who built them. However, Jackson particularly detailed the fictionalized hacienda where Ramona grew up and the small adobes where the couple lived. She also described other native dwellings from the simple brush type to the adobe *jacals* and wood structures that the Anglo settlers virtually stole from the natives — along with capturing the adobe haciendas and ranchos of the *Californios* and *Mexicanos* — as the newcomers staked claims or presented indisputable U.S. purchase records of the property.

Jackson's *Ramona* depicts what is called the "Franciscan version" of history, as opposed to the "Anglo version." According to the novel, the missions were peaceful havens for the natives, which was not always accurate, and the interloping Anglos and the U.S. bureaucratic system were solely at fault for the demise of the California natives and the end of the Spanish-Mexican way of life. *Ramona* aroused public sentiment for improving the natives' conditions and Jackson's book is considered alongside Harriet Beecher Stowe's *Uncle Tom's Cabin* as one of the two great ethical novels of the century.

A Southern California Difference

Of the Alta California settlement, the Spanish missions in Southern California were the most densely settled. They were more prosperous and older than those north of the Tehachapi River, which became the dividing line between the north and south of the coastal region. Franciscan missionaries referred to the missions north of Santa Barbara as "worthless skeletons," and during Alta California's brief Mexican rule (1821-49), a proposal for dividing the state in two was made at the first session of the Mexican legislature in 1822. Less than a decade following statehood, in 1859, two-thirds of the people of Southern California forwarded to the United States Congress a measure for division of the new state into two parts; only the outbreak of the Civil War prohibited what was certainly a division of the new state. In later years, this sense of division would persist in formal developments, and the greatest movement for the revival of colonial styles would dominate the southern portion of the state, particularly from San Diego up to Santa Barbara.

PART FOUR

MISSION REVIVAL, 1885-1915

ADVOCATES AND AESTHETES

The decade of the 1880s, when Helen Hunt Jackson came to California, was a "boom" time. Continuing through the 1910s, growth in population, tourism and wealth abounded, along with occasional over-speculation and decline. As earlier developments would die out, they would lay the groundwork and set up the infrastructure for later periods of commercial and population growth. At the same time, there was a popular desire to discover an architectural style that would be considered indigenous to California, and subsequently the Mission Revival caught on with a vengeance, especially in the *Ramona* territory of Southern California.

Although the missions were few, did not exhibit a consistent style, and promoted the Spanish-Franciscan aspect of the heritage rather than that of the Mexican peasant, Victorian developers, builders and architects could use the idealized missions to produce a unique but traditional architecture that would be identified with the region.

The term "Mission Revival," covering specific works from the approximate period of 1885 to 1915, is a later designation from the 1950s and 1960s. It defines one of the richest of California's Spanish-Mexican-Native American cultural revivals, better known today for its conceptual bases and theoretical thinking than for the scarce number of remaining Mission Revival buildings.

These mission style structures are easily identified by their common use of two highly imagistic decorative elements: the scalloped Mission Order gable, and the bell tower, often composed of a series of larger to smaller squares and sometimes topped with a low dome. However, there were a number of ways that the missions were inspiring without copying them in decorative detail: the large-scale, undecorated walls, arched entrances, *portales* and low, tiled roofs were virtual building blocks for modern structures that would appear many years later.

During the real estate promotion period of the 1880s to the 1910s, most of the missions were preserved in some manner. If they weren't restored in an archaeological sense, they were cleaned up and put in order for tourists. Their preservation is primarily the result — not of the commercial promoters — but of serious, altruistic advocates like Helen Hunt Jackson, whose publications had ushered in the Mission Revival. Jackson's California-theme books helped the young state to bridge from the cultural exoticism of the Victorians to the intelligent scholarly approach of largely self-taught ethnologists, historians and aesthetes who were drawn like Jackson to the southern portion of the state.

One such character was Charles Fletcher Lummis, who can now be considered a leading proponent of the Mission Revival. He was from Lynn, Massachusetts, and had attended Harvard with Theodore Roosevelt. It was 1881, when he had just graduated, married and was living in Cincinnati, Ohio that he struck a deal with Harrison Gray Otis, the publisher of the *Los Angeles Times*: he would walk out west from Ohio to Los Angeles, and would write a series of articles about his trek and his impression of the city if Otis would give him a job at the *Times*. On the journey, Lummis studied the Native American cultures of the Southwest and on his arrival, Otis gave him the job of city editor.

Lummis was charismatic and energetic. He founded several groundbreaking ethnic preservation groups: the Arroyo Seco Foundation (begun 1885) to preserve the natural arroyo setting and local native homes in the lush cliffs of the Pasadena area; the Sequoya League (1902), founded particularly to aid 300 local natives evicted from Warner Ranch and relocated to government lands; and the Southwest Museum (begun 1910) to preserve the arts and heritage of the Southwest Native Americans.

In 1888, Lummis formed the Association for the Preservation of the Missions (renamed the Landmarks Club in 1895) which began the restoration of the San Gabriel and San Fernando missions, and Olvera Street, the oldest street of structures in Los Angeles. To promote the preservation of the missions, and the causes and arts of the local natives, he started and, from 1894 to 1916, he edited his magazine *Land of Sunshine*, later called *Outwest*.

RAILROADS AND REAL ESTATE

Californians claimed a noble history with the missions as landmarks of civilization and worn images of strength. Together, aesthetes and writers — like Lummis and Jackson — who were interested in local history, and city boosters and real estate promoters, who were interested in enticing settlers and tourists agreed upon reviving the missions. They helped each other's causes in the swell of population growth and tourism.

Victimized by secularization in 1834 and the loss of their land, animals and crops, the missions became the romanticized cause for the new period of cultural exoticism and preservation, while at the same time using them as tourist attractions. As well, both the Native Americans and the Spaniards were rediscovered as the heritage of Southern California, although the facts of the heritage were idealized and falsified. Real estate promoters drew upon the missions, the falsified ethnic heritage and revived the mission architecture to lure settlers and tourists to the young state.

During the significant 1883-1910 growth phase, the real estate boom of 1887 was ignited by the completion of the Santa Fe railroad line. After a price war with the Southern Pacific, Santa Fe offered such low fares that it brought out millions of tourists and settlers to the Pacific Coast, and numbers of opportunists came to Southern California to make a living or simply enjoy a better year-round climate. A number of mid-Westerners organized tours to visit parts of Southern California after 1900 and for the following two decades, Los Angeles was essentially a tourist town.

The character of Jackson's *Ramona* became the focus for all kinds of real estate and railroad promotions after 1887. Postcards depicted — and trains would stop at — places where Ramona was fictionally born, lived and married Alessandro. *Ramona* continued to promote tourist interest in the missions, while more books were written on the missions, and in 1912, John Steven McGroaty wrote *The Mission Play* about the same themes as Jackson's — praising the Native Americans, the Spanish governors and the Franciscan padres. In its first year, McGroaty's play was performed for over two million

Opposite page
The Mission Order gable, entrance arcade and bell towers of the Riverside Public Library, 1903, are Missio n Revival elements that are handsomely assembled for the facade by the firm of Burnham and Bliesner. The style was dignified and its scale was suitable for such public structures.

Below
Mission Revival elements could create interesting compositions and their use on individual residences imparted great presence and prestige, as seen in the Powers Residence, 1905, by A.L. Haley. The house is located in a Victorian neighborhood in Los Angeles where the style was a clever departure from the bric-a-brac of the past while its ornate windows and towers still appear Victorian in our time.

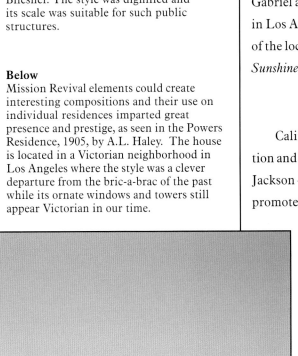

people at the San Gabriel Mission. Its production is an institutional tourist attraction to this day, along with theatrical productions of *Ramona*.

City Promotions and Mission Style Cities

The earlier booms of the 1870s and 1880s had been primarily railroad promotions, but in the 1900s came the first local city promotions. City leaders and developers built housing and infrastructures, such as paved and curbed roads, piped water and irrigation systems. They even helped to establish the universities and institutions that would remain a part of Southern California, and the Mission Revival style worked best for the larger public buildings where the original scale of the missions could be matched to some extent.

Promoting the mission myth in the Los Angeles area, was an impressive roster of leaders, among them was General Harrison Gray Otis, publisher of the *Los Angeles Times*, who began the Los Angeles Chamber of Commerce, E.P. Clark, originally of Montana, who gave the city public and educational buildings, E.L. Doheny, who developed oil in the area, Senator John P. Jones of Nevada who established Santa Monica, and Henry E. Huntington, who created Redondo Beach among other developments. Many beach cities like Hermosa Beach, a 1902 family resort, included mission style structures, such as homes, hotels, boardwalks, amusements parks, bathhouses, auditoriums, and dance halls.

Mission Revival style came to be used for many new building types, from motels to motion picture studios. In addition to the railroads, growth of cities depended on new highways, streets and local electric trains, and transportation systems frequently used the style for their terminal buildings. The Southern Pacific and the Santa Fe railroads built their Southwest and California stations in the mission style, such as Bakewell and Brown's 1914 Santa Fe Railroad depot at San Diego, an over-scaled mission facade with two side towers at the entrance and a forecourt area resembling an enclosed *atrio*. For the local electric cars of the Los Angeles area, the Pacific Electric substations, circa 1900, were a simple church form with Mission Order gable ends.

Of the many Mission Revival tourist hotels were the original sections of the Beverly Hills Hotel, 1910-12, by Elmer Grey, the Byron Springs Resort Hotel, circa 1910, by James M. Reid, east of Oakland, Frederick Roehrig's Green Hotel, in Pasadena, from the 1890s, with an added annex and a Moorish porte cochere. Most famous is the Mission Inn, Riverside (originally the Glenwood Inn), first designed in 1890-1901 by Arthur Benton, who propagandized the Mission Revival in architectural journals. The Mission Inn's later renovations and additions by Myron Hunt, Elmer Grey, and Stanley Wilson, included a Cloister added in 1910 and Spanish Wings in 1914. It continued to be added to until it covered an entire block. At the entrance, it emphasized the mission aspect with the Mission Order gable but formally it mixed in Moorish and Italianate elements. Today it's much changed and the original curbside mission wall is replaced.

Whole towns were designed in mission style, including Planada, which was planned as pure Mission Revival by A.H. Stibolt and W.D. Cook in 1911. Even Naples originally had mission style buildings designed by Norman F. Marsh and Robert E. Marsh, 1904, although it had Italian bridges and canals. Riverside remodeled its commercial area and added numerous Mission Revival structures, including Burnham & Bliesner's Riverside Public Library, 1903, which has a nice combination of sym-

The Mission Revival that lasted from approximately 1885 to 1915 was well-grounded in the history of the region and produced many public buildings that aided in real estate and tourist promotions. The Green Hotel in Pasadena, 1898-1903, designed by Frederick Roehrig has Moorish domes and decorative elements that relate it to the Victorian phase of the movement.

metrical bell towers with domed tops and a scalloped Mission Order gable that is set back, allowing the lower arcade and *portal* to form the base of a second-story balcony.

MISSION STYLE ELEMENTS

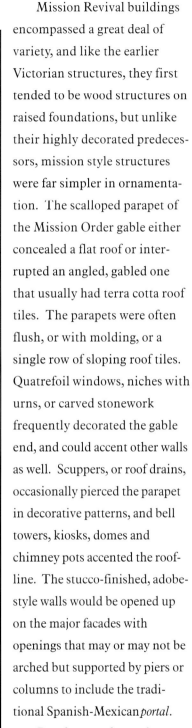

Mission Revival buildings encompassed a great deal of variety, and like the earlier Victorian structures, they first tended to be wood structures on raised foundations, but unlike their highly decorated predecessors, mission style structures were far simpler in ornamentation. The scalloped parapet of the Mission Order gable either concealed a flat roof or interrupted an angled, gabled one that usually had terra cotta roof tiles. The parapets were often flush, or with molding, or a single row of sloping roof tiles. Quatrefoil windows, niches with urns, or carved stonework frequently decorated the gable end, and could accent other walls as well. Scuppers, or roof drains, occasionally pierced the parapet in decorative patterns, and bell towers, kiosks, domes and chimney pots accented the roofline. The stucco-finished, adobe-style walls would be opened up on the major facades with openings that may or may not be arched but supported by piers or columns to include the traditional Spanish-Mexican *portal*.

Portales, corredors and entrance porches were prominent features of Mission Revival buildings, and usually these porches were one-story, open and, if not confined to the entry, may run across the full width of the facade, and may extend to incorporate a side carport in small houses. In two-story buildings, a terrace might crown the porch. Practical decorations of the period would sometime include striped awnings over windows and doors.

Although most mission style structures were of stucco to mimic the adobe look of the original adobes, arroyo stones and boulder rock details often accompanied many

Mission Revival works — sometimes as a retaining wall and trim and, most often as boulder fireplaces on many Mission Revival interiors. One of the most fanciful stone designs was Arthur Benton's Switzer's Chapel, 1924, with the stonework meant to appear as an extension of its Arroyo Seco cliff location. The chapel was part of Commodore Switzer's retreats — tiny wood and stone cabins reached by burro.

VICTORIAN PHASE, 1885-1905

In the 1880s, many Mission Revival structures simply grafted more ornate elements onto the typical Victorian building, making the Queen Anne Moorish style popular. "Moorish" elements were sometimes called "Turkish" and the use of the decorative forms continued the romantic exoticism of the previous decades.

The mission syle with a dramatic Moorish flavor became popular for cultural palaces and exposition buildings, such as the Pasadena Grand Opera House, 1888-89, attributed to Alonzo M. Grey, and the California Midwinter International Exposition, 1894, in San Francisco which had included Samuel Newsom's Agricultural and Horticultural Building.

However, in residential work, the Mission Revival proportions and details did not translate well, but were adapted nonetheless with the Mission Order gable appearing somewhat pompous and ridiculous on the smaller, single-family house. An example is the 1905 Powers Residence by A.L. Haley in a former Victorian suburban community in Los Angeles. The highly decorative ornament is restrained to certain key areas and outlines. Above the first floor entrance porch, the Mission Order gable is decorated with a central oculus. Differently scaled side towers flank the gable and the entrance porch wraps around one side of the house — both towers and side porch adding to a well-balanced but asymmetrical design.

The grandiose Mission Order gable and flanking bell towers were also used in the Mission Revival house of artist Paul de Longpre, by L.L. Bourgeois, 1900, formerly in Hollywood. Described at the time as in the "Moorish-Mission style of architecture which is always artistic and eminently appropriate for a California house," Bourgeois actually applied decorative ornament to carefully delineated borders — both on the exterior and interior.

ARTS AND CRAFTS PHASE, 1905-1915

Charles Lummis, through his organizations and his magazine, did much to connect the Mission Revival to the theories, concepts and creative developments of the American Arts and Crafts movement and, specifically, to Southern California's own Arroyo Culture which supported the movement's decorative arts, painting, handcrafts, furniture and architecture.

In keeping with Lummis' highly personal interpretation of Arts and Crafts principles, his own house which he began in 1895, was purposefully primitive. Local Isleta Indians helped him drag up arroyo boulders to build it. The front boulder-faced facade features a side detail with a Mission Order gable and a round tower. The rear facade is stuccoed and displays that the roof is actually shingled, unlike most tile-roofed mission structures. Inside, the house is rustic with log ceiling beams and concrete-and-stone floors. There are built-in cabinets, carefully honed wood doors and primitive decorative details for the hardware and fireplace decoration. Lummis' tight group of Arroyo friends and Arts and Crafts followers participated in its decoration. Some of the metalwork was designed by artist Maynard Dixon, the decoration of one bedroom fireplace was by sculptor Gutzon Borglum, and built-in throughout were memorabilia and crafts from Lummis' trips to South America.

Since mission revivalists paid close attention to the decorative arts of interior decoration, they liked simple, rudimentary furniture, and particularly the heavy, simple-lined oak furniture of Gustav Stickley. They felt that his designs, that have come to be known as "Mission" furniture, appropriately belonged in Mission style structures. Stickley, who headed the east coast-based Arts and Crafts movement published the California works of Lummis and his friends in his magazine, the *Craftsman*, while Lummis published the works of Stickley in his California magazine, *Land of Sunshine/Outwest*.

Like Lummis, many designers, architects and craftpersons of the Mission Revival belonged to the Arroyo group and believed in returning to the earlier time of the missions and the native population. They advocated reviving to the simple, natural life where handcraft and living close to nature was of greatest importance. They also were concerned about building craft technology as it related to concepts of morality and democracy, similar to the philosophical concerns of the American and English Arts and Crafts followers.

Unlike the European Arts and Crafts followers, most American followers believed in using new technologies. One of the Arroyo group, writer George Wharton James, wrote in 1903 that Los Angeles architect Lester S. Moore was "one of the earliest to see and appreciate the possibilities of the Mission style" for his use of concrete. However, there were several Mission Revival concrete buildings constructed earlier, such as the 1889 Amphitheater on the Chautauqua grounds at Redondo Beach displaying the concrete pattern of the board forms. Architects Charles F. Whittlesey and Harrison Albright were also using reinforced concrete in the 1900s and concrete began to be associated with the Mission Revival — its rough forms mimicking the crudity of Mission Era adobe bricks.

Irving Gill celebrated the formal simplicity of the Mission Revival while at the same time praising the technological development of concrete. He was a turn of the century progressive, committed to using the latest materials and building methods, and yet, true to the Arts and Crafts sensibility, Gill felt a deep sense of responsibility to reflect culture at its best and to return to fundamentals. In his writings and in his work, he was romantic about Southern California's unspoiled landscape and found inspiration in the mission heritage.

Gill believed that architects would take an important role in reshaping the built environment of California although he had only come to the state in 1893, after working in the Chicago "skyscraper" firm of Adler and Sullivan. While his early work in the

Opposite page
Artist Paul de Longpre turned his 1900 mission-style residence on three Hollywood acres into a tourist destination. It presented a symmetrical arrangement of Mission Revival elements, including three Mission Order gables, two bell towers and an entrance arcade. As a fashionable expression of the local history, the style was an excellent promotional form and de Longpre's enormous rose garden attracted sales for his flower paintings.

Charismatic and unique, Charles Fletcher Lummis promoted California's Arts and Crafts movement, its mission history, early adobes, and an appreciation for native cultures. His own Pasadena arroyo-area residence, 1895+, defies stylistic categories, however, it features a Mission Order gable and a tower on its stone-faced facade, associating it with the Mission Revival.

San Diego area is associated with the Mission Revival, he later developed his own cubist modern style, synthesizing the mission style into contemporary architecture and using unadorned block forms and simple arches abstracted from the mission vocabulary. Also, deriving landscape aspects from the mission tradition, Gill would extend his structures into the landscape by means of walled courtyards and pergolas. His roof trellises covered walkways and created outdoor garden rooms.

Gill began to use the mission imagery in 1904 and the 1908 St. James Chapel (now First Baptist Church) in La Jolla is the most correct of its expression where he imitated the thickness of the adobe wall in concrete and gave the facade a Mission Order gable in very simple, smooth outline form. Later, Gill's Torrance Railroad Station, 1913, also incorporates the Mission Order gable shape in such a modified, simplified manner that it appears extremely modern and abstract. His Bailey House, 1907, La Jolla, had Craftsman interiors, like other Mission Revival works, in which wide redwood paneling was hand-polished. The simple furnishings were built-in or rustic freestanding pieces Gill had designed. His wood cupboards and natural stained doors were detailed with multiple panels and spare flush ornament.

Most of Gill's houses are a simple combination of cubes and arches, abstracting the missions to their key elements and thereby expressing unadorned Modern Movement design. Gill's synthesis is seen in the La Jolla Woman's Club, 1914, the Scripps House, 1916, La Jolla; and the apartments of the Horatio West Court, 1919, Santa Monica.

Similarly cubist but mission-inspired structures included an unbuilt urban skyscraper that Gill designed, called the Casa Grande, 1915, as well as architect John Parkinson's house for himself, Los Angeles, circa 1906, and Mead and Requa's Krotona Court, Los Angeles, 1921. The Mission Revival style was used for the central tower of Bertram Goodhue and Carleton Winslow, Sr.'s Los Angeles Public Library, 1925, and even the blocky Prairie School form of the Wrigley Mansion by Arthur Stimson, in Pasadena, 1911, reflected the solid, massive shape that related many similar upscale homes to the California missions.

The St. James Chapel, now First Baptist Church La Jolla, was a Mission Revival chapel designed by Irving Gill in 1908. Gill reduced the style's formal elements to basic shapes while showing the fundamental strength of mission architecture, particularly its majestic gable and basilica structural form.

Gill's pergola of the Woman's Club is upheld by double columns set up on bases. The pergola was a form by which Gill grounded his work in nature and extended his structures into the landscape, just as the missions had.

La Jolla Woman's Club, 1914, shows how Irving Gill developed abstractions of the Mission Revival style, such as the arcaded *portal*, and the attached pergola which could provide a mission courtyard experience on a small suburban lot. The tiered fountain also adds to the mission character.

A Note about Northern California Mission Revival

The 1886-91 Palo Alto campus of Leland Stanford Junior University displayed the influence of the Mission Revival in the master plan and general character of the buildings. Spanish names are still used for the dormitories and streets, and Spanish colonization is the theme for the frieze of the Memorial Arch. Architects Shepley, Rutan and Coolidge adapted the revival to the weighty detail of the Richardsonian Romanesque, borrowing the then-current trend of architect Henry Hobson Richardson's Boston and Chicago public works. For the inner quadrangle, Charles Coolidge applied Richardson's Romanesque detail of rusticated masonry, grouped arches, and squat columns to a heavy mission design of a one-story format, with tile roof and arcades.

In the San Francisco Bay area, Willis Polk and John Galen Howard also aided the Mission Revival, influenced by the Stanford buildings and the Richardsonian Romanesque. They collaborated on a set of articles on the missions and published their sketches along with works of Samuel Newsom and Ernest A. Coxhead. Other articles sanctioned a typically California design for the California Building at the upcoming 1893 Columbian Exposition in Chicago. A competition was held and the Mission Style was favored, finally preferring A. Page Brown's eclectic assemblage of mission elements, including a dome and an old mission belfry. Brown's design drew heavily on the ideas of others and caused resentment among the architects. It incorporated Samuel Newsom's proposal of 1891 using superimposed Mission Order gable facades for all entrances. Bernard Maybeck designed the dominant center dome and went to Chicago for Brown's office to supervise construction. Brown's only original idea seemed to be the mission arcade as the linear core of the building.

CHAPTER TWO

MANY CENTURIES, MANY STYLES
IMPORTED SOURCES FOR CALIFORNIA'S SPANISH REVIVAL, 1915-1940

REINVENTING SPANISH PERIOD STYLES

In the 1890s through 1910s, both sophisticated clients and designers were broadening their taste through travel and education and, by 1915, an educated historicist phase of period styles spread across the country. The general population of America appreciated works that had sophistication and foreign-based ornamental detail. Alongside Tudor, Italianate and French Normandy designs, Spanish style works arose in great abundance, particularly in Southern California, where people used it to claim their tentative lineage as an Hispanic colony.

Mansions and bungalows, country clubs and filling stations, city halls and dance halls were designed in the ubiquitous Spanish Revival style, also referred to academically and more correctly as the Spanish Colonial Revival. While Northern California produced numbers of the style, its major architects who had expressed Spanish leanings — Maybeck, Coxhead, Polk and Howard — developed unique expressions of their own making. On the other hand, Julia Morgan worked in the central and southern regions, producing some fine Spanish style works for her major client, William Randolph Hearst. Southern California, with its milder Spanish Mediterranean type climate, took the lead in the Spanish Revival. Its architects, designers and city leaders became major proponents of the style.

Unlike the Mission Revival, which based its forms on idealized versions of local Spanish and Mexican buildings, Spanish Colonial Revival architects and clients looked overseas to Spain to take forms and elements from the rich wealth of centuries of styles. They perpetuated an unstated cultural myth and romantic fiction that California was the New Spain of North America after only seventy-nine to eighty years of limited Spanish-Mexican contact: approximately fifty-two years under Spanish Franciscan colonization with innumerable Anglo pioneers settling the region, and approximately twenty-eight years under a chaotic Mexican rule shared with Anglo overpopulation. The myth gave Anglo Californians a European past and pedigree.

Prestige was one good reason to adopt the European Spanish style. Millionaire newspaper publisher William Randolph Hearst first adopted the style for his Los Angeles Examiner Building, 1914, designed by San Francisco-based architect Julia Morgan and local architect J. Martyn Haenke of Haenke and Dodd. Morgan studied at the Ecole des Beaux Arts in Paris and the body of her work generally tended to Italian and Spanish designs, and she freely assembled them with medieval and classical English and French elements.

The Examiner building has mission aspects and is transitional to the Spanish Revival period styles. The entire building is like a palace compound taking almost an entire city block and the interior *Plateresco*-styled lobby with its elaborate staircases also gives the impression of palatial architecture. The central entrance block is marked by a scalloped Mission Order gable and behind it a double-story structure — a broad drum and dome crowned with a cupola — flanked by small bell towers. The ends of the long entrance block were also marked by colorful tiled, domed bell-towers. Across the front facade was an arcade, originally in-filled with glass to allow viewing the printing presses.

The formal birth date of the new style came a year later, in 1915, when San Diego city leaders opened the doors for the Panama-California Exposition. While the then-local Irving Gill had already started designing modern buildings based on local mission forms for the fair, his designs were rejected for the ornate Spanish Baroque

The first notable Spanish Colonial Revival building in Southern California was the Los Angeles Examiner Building, 1914, by San Francisco-based architect Julia Morgan with J. Martyn Haenke of Haenke and Dodd as the local architect. Morgan, who studied at the Ecole des Beaux Arts, Paris, designed this for her chief client, publisher William Randolph Hearst. True to the historical eclecticism of the revival, she incorporated a Mission Order gable and Moorish domes, as well as Italianate and other Western European elements in the overall design.

style, "imported," as it were, by the eastern establishment in the form of New York-Boston architects Bertram Goodhue and Carleton Winslow. Providing inspiration for other lavishly ornamented Spanish buildings, the exposition's lavish California Building and other structures were part-*Plateresco* and part-*Churrigueresco* — and when they were described the affected French terms "Plateresque" and "Churrigueresque" were employed rather than the Spanish.

The strength of the Mission Revival dwelt in its theoretical ties with the American Arts and Crafts movement and its solid relationship to the local mission architecture, albeit based on archaeologically-incorrect versions of what was actually a *vernacular* style. However, the more sophisticated Spanish Colonial Revival architects and designers had no interest in theoretical grounding and roots in the true California or Spanish culture. These later Spanish style proponents were consumed with an urbane American cultural attitude based on an educated academic body of defined period styles, of which Spanish was merely one European variant with many sub-categories. Any European style was valid in a land composed of immigrants, and those styles that were carefully studied or skillfully portrayed in a contemporary manner were considered the best. The justification of California's Spanish heritage was a nice addition for those who either wanted to perpetuate the mythic heritage or realized the appropriateness of the design elements for the California climate and landscape.

Designers produced all of the Spanish sub-categories in their revival. There was Moorish/Gothic, Andalusian vernacular, Classical-*Desornamentado*, *Plateresco* and *Churrigueresco* styles. Most often a Spanish Revival structure would have multiple period references and could have additional local Monterey features and other Anglo details. In terms of Spanish style public and private gardens, designers and landscapers would frequently mix Moorish and Italianate elements which they associated with the formal gardens at the Alhambra and vernacular gardens of Spanish farmhouses, where both European parterres and Moorish flush-to-the-ground water channels would create major axes. Many times a full Italianate garden accompanied Spanish Revival designs, showing a preference for the long axes of parterres and terraced spaces compared to the tiled rivulets of the Moorish tradition.

City Planning, Contractor Casas and Courtyard Apartments

Between 1915 and 1925, over fifteen California towns were built or rebuilt to a uniform period style, and most of these towns were in the southern portion of the state and most were in Spanish Revival style. City planners and city leaders spurred by the pride and promotions of the earlier growth periods, locked into the current ideas of the fictional Spanish heritage, based on the mere fifty-two years of colonization and a scattering of vernacular native-built Spanish buildings.

California's four Spanish military *presidios* were planned according to the points of the compass in the tradition of the Law of the Indies and Spain's royal ordinance. However, the missions and pueblos were usually built over native villages and conformed to the natural contours and exploited the major elements of existing vegetation and landscape of hills, beaches, or desert areas. The 1920s Spanish Revival projects followed the latter practice.

One of the first in the Spanish planning movement was the redesign of the city of Nordhoff to change it from Anglo pioneer style to Spanish. Originally named after

The birth of the Spanish Colonial Revival in California occurred in 1915 with the opening of the Panama-California Exposition in San Diego. The *Churrigueresco*-style California Quadrangle was the original entrance to the fair and the California Tower and Administration Building, now the Museum of Man, was the work of New York architects Bertram Goodhue and Carleton Winslow. (Irving Gill began the fair project in 1911, however, his minimalist designs based on the region's missions were dismissed for the imported vision of Baroque Spain presented by Goodhue and Winslow.)

City planning throughout Southern California was impacted by the Spanish Revival. Rancho Santa Fe — like Palos Verdes, San Clemente, Ojai and Santa Barbara — was designed to appear like a Spanish village with white adobe-like buildings, red tile roofs and walled courtyards. In 1924, architect Lillian Rice, of the San Diego firm of Mead and Requa, began the design for the Santa Fe Railroad as a rural retreat.

Charles Nordhoff, who was renowned for his writings on natural living, it was re-named Ojai after the name of the valley and its original Spanish land grant. Edmund Libbey, founder of the glass company, bought the city center and hired San Diego architects Frank Mead and Richard Requa in 1916 to redesign the main street with a Spanish arched *portal* to front the shops. The architects included a prominent post office with a tower based on a tiled Spanish *Plateresco*-styled one from the Columbus Cathedral in Havana, and they designed the main street entrance to a seven and a half-acre park with pergolas and low adobe walls with some Mission Order arches, like those at the original Mission Inn at Riverside.

Like Ojai, the Spanish style community of Palos Verdes was also first planned in the 1910s but was completed in the 1920s. New York banker Frank A. Vanderlip acquired sixteen thousand acres comprising most of the entire Palos Verdes Peninsula. He hired landscape architects Olmsted and Olmsted, Howard Shaw and Myron Hunt to lay out a "millionaire's colony" which was meant to include residential estates, parks, clubs, roads, three model villages and four commercial centers. World War I halted the development but after the war a scheme one fifth the size of the original was master planned in 1922-23 by Olmsted and Olmsted, along with the talented architect, planner and writer Charles H. Cheney.

Spanish was the official architectural style of the residential community and an Art Jury was established to review all additional designs. The one commercial center that was finished, Malaga Cove, 1922-25, was designed by Webber, Staunton and Spaulding. The stone-surfaced *Plateresco-Churrigueresco* design is organized around a parking plaza lined with two- and three-story arcaded buildings for shops and restaurants with offices above. A corner fountain installed in 1930 was copied after a sixteenth-century one in Bologna, Italy and its Mediterranean design and stone

surface suit the Spanish plaza. From the Malaga Cove complex, a passthrough with Spanish *Mudéjar*-like stonework bridges the street that leads from the plaza to the hillside Palos Verdes Public Library and park which is graced with live peacocks. Myron Hunt and H.C. Chambers designed the Spanish Revival library project, along with another Andalusian-style work nearby, the home of Frederick Law Olmsted, Jr.

The most comprehensive Spanish-style community is Rancho Santa Fe, located twenty-five miles north of San Diego. It is on the Spanish land grant Rancho San Dieguito that, in 1906, was bought by the Santa Fe Railroad as a place to raise eucalyptus trees for railroad ties. The trees turned out to be unsuitable to hold the necessary spikes, so it was decided to make the land a rural retreat with citrus groves. In 1924 Lillian Rice of Mead and Requa's San Diego office began the project and eventually took it over for her busy partners. Rice created a tiny, idealized one- and two-story Spanish village in a rural environment with a single hotel, a small commercial center and Spanish adobe town homes and casas arranged around the Y formation of the major avenues of the town. It was meant to attract retired businessmen and fruit growers and be a second home community for an upper middle class. It ended up attracting serious Hollywood players to the surrounding acreage. Bing Crosby bought and remodeled the old land grant adobe and Douglas Fairbanks, Sr. and Mary Pickford established their 800-acre Rancho Zorro adjacent to the town.

Factions in Santa Barbara, a Spanish *presidio* town, wanted to retain the Spanish heritage as early as 1874, when an article in the *Santa Barbara Press* remarked about "maintaining the landmarks and charming characteristics against improvements." Successive decades managed to set in place solid ways that sentiment could be implemented. In 1909 a Civic League was formed and engaged a city planner, and in 1920 the Santa Barbara Community Arts Association, a private group, set up planning and architectural controls. After a 1925 earthquake, city planning efforts were stepped up and in 1930 the first comprehensive zoning ordinance was adopted by the city, limiting the heights of commercial and residential structures. By 1939, Santa Barbara was the first American city to set up an architectural review board and in 1947, the board was officially established by the city council. Only Hispanic and Mediterranean traditions were allowed and the goal was to retain Santa Barbara's existing Spanish charm.

The arched entranceway of the Santa Barbara County Courthouse is made to appear like a Roman triumphal arch. The building's heroic scale is quite appealing but in 1929 it was criticized by architect-planner-writer Charles Cheney in his *Californian Architecture in Santa Barbara*. "Romance ran riot in the new Court House," he wrote. "It has an extraordinary number of intriguing bits of design, even if the scale is too large, too forced to seem to belong to the happy intimate style of Santa Barbara."

The Santa Barbara County Courthouse, 1927-29, by William Mooser and J. William Hersey, is a monumental Spanish courtyard compound that followed the local demand for Spanish- and Mediterranean-style buildings first made by individuals and historic organizations and continued to this day by the city's Architectural Review Board. The entrance appears somewhat mission-like with a decorated stonework entrance, a quatrefoil window and a large bell-and-clock tower.

The L-planned Santa Barbara County Courthouse is actually several linked buildings: a courtroom-office block, a hall of records and a jail. They all face the immense terraced and sunken garden originally designed by Ralph T. Stevens.

Potential homebuilders were enticed to build their own "casa California" by the many newspaper ads for Spanish-style home builders and by house plan books that proliferated throughout Southern California in the 1920s and 1930s. As well, suburban communities of tract houses offered a bit of Spain and Mexico, even if they were inter-spersed with New England cottages and English Tudor and French Provincial designs.

The 1925 earthquake, occurring during the height of the Spanish Colonial Revival movement, resulted in rebuilding the destroyed Santa Barbara County Courthouse in the Spanish Revival style. The large 1927-29 courtyard compound is by architects William Mooser and J. William Hersey and is generally considered the best public monument of the movement. It's befitting other public works by the leading Santa Barbara Spanish revivalists, such as the El Paseo, 1922-23, a village of shops and courtyards by James Osborne Craig, as well as George Washington Smith's Lobero Theater, 1922-24, and the Arlington-Fox Theatre and shopping area, 1929, by William Edwards and Joseph Plunkett.

There were also other Spanish city identities created and re-created in the same Spanish styles at San Clemente, Montecito, Palm Springs, Fullerton, Pacific Palisades and Pasadena. San Diego, La Jolla and Coronado went through their Spanish renovations at the time of the Panama-California Exposition. While Los Angeles never had a major Spanish city overhaul, it certainly had its Spanish style communities like Leimert Park and the early Bel-Air works of Mark Daniels and Elmer Grey.

In addition to entire towns and individual homes and public buildings of the 1920s and 1930s, California's Spanish style house plans were frequently sold from books produced by contractors and builders for individuals to build their own casas. There were plenty of new tracts of suburban houses and apartment houses.

One example of a Los Angeles 1920s tract development, Westwood, included period designs of primarily two types — the popular Spanish casa and the English style cottage — and they were designed by a stable of talented architects including Wallace Neff, Gordon Kaufmann, P.P. Lewis and Allen Siple. The Westwood tracts showed the clever manner in which the casa could be fitted to its small suburban setting and yet still include a courtyard on the lot, and the abbreviated forms of a tower, a *portal*, a *Mudéjar*-style balcony and a tile fountain and iron grill entrance gate.

Other contractors and builders would use the Spanish styles for apartment houses and the most popular was the courtyard type apartment which provided the opportunity to plan the dwellings around a communal court or green space with fountains of various types. The apartments built by one couple, Arthur and Nina Zwebell, provide excellent examples of the type. They built eight courtyard apartments, of which six are Spanish Revival styles. Three of their most successful were the Villa Primavera — a Spanish-Mexican hacienda design (despite its picturesque Italian name, it was also called Mexican Village), the Patio del Moro, a Moorish style courtyard (with Spanish-Moorish elements), and the Andalusia Apartments, named after the province which inspired the majority of Spanish designs in Southern California.

Arthur Zwebell designed the structures and Nina Zwebell's interior services included Spanish Revival furniture, wrought iron curtain rods and embroidered linen sheets. The Zwebells' works also show how the loosely-interpreted copy-book method worked successfully, and sometimes produced exact copies, as a tile-embellished, double-arched balcony window at the Andalusia was directly copied from a Cordoban one illustrated in a then-current book by Arthur and Mildred Byne, their 1924 *Spanish Gardens and Patios*.

The Andalusia Apartments best exemplifies the Spanish Colonial Revival style applied to this building type. In the courtyard, a Moorish-style fireplace and a tile quatrefoil fountain, corner tower and wooden balconies are forms derived from the vernacular buildings found in the Spanish province. Presenting a singular building with a forecourt flanked by low side wings (actually garages) at the street, the Andalusia virtually hides the interior courtyard and the apartment units themselves, in keeping with both Spanish and Mexican methods of privacy.

The source for the courtyard apartments was ultimately the Spanish *cortijo* farm which Southern California missions and ranchos had continued. As early as the 1880s, the Spanish organizational tradition had influenced apartment courts, becoming extremely popular in the 1920s with the Zwebells and others.

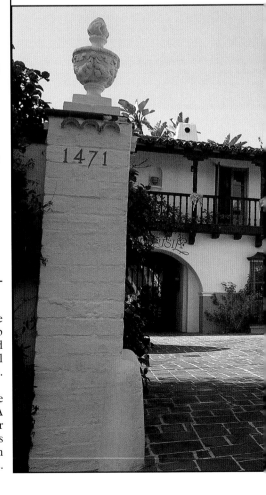

Top: Among the Spanish-style courtyard apartments built in the Los Angeles area in the 1920s, the Villa Primavera (also called the Mexican Village) was the first apartment group built by Arthur and Nina Zwebell in 1923. An arched entrance leads to the central courtyard from which each apartment is entered. Elements like the individual patios, left, and the wall color — like natural adobe — give the compound a Mexican appearance.

Bottom: Named after the Spanish province, the Andalusia Apartments, 1926, were the Zwebell's third apartment group and its planning and authentic detail make it their best. A front balcony overlooks the parking court created by garage side wings. The arched door leads to a lush interior courtyard. The Zwebells — who designed the interior furnishings as well as the buildings — influenced regional architects and builders to build in the Spanish courtyard form with ingenious floor plans and delightful tile and woodwork details.

SOURCES OF SPANISH PERIOD STYLES

California's fifty-two year period of Spanish-Franciscan cultural impact and the following brief Mexican period brought in piecemeal elements of the Spanish period styles. The formal influence was merely a high style detail here and there among the vernacular mission buildings and adobes. In fact, the slim amount of stylistic influence that would be truly Spanish and brought into the region by the Franciscans was a complex, multi-ethnic cultural impact — part-Spanish and part-Islamic in its origins. California's development was further compounded by the twenty-eight year rule of multi-ethnic Mexican culture — part-Spanish, part-Native American in its origins. From the late eighteenth century, California's large Anglo pioneer population would have further complicated the cultural influences to the styles of the region.

Therefore, in the Spanish Colonial Revival period, sources could be broad and loosely interpreted. Each architect and educated client developed his or her favorite formal Spanish repertoire and some were inspired by buildings seen in travels to Spain, Mexico or Spain's former Central and South American colonies. However, both architects and clients tended to like examples clearly based on Spanish European designs and not Mexican or South American interpretations of original Spanish structures.

Californians learned about Spain's history of architecture and decorative designs from a high volume of American published black-and-white source books popular during the 1910s and 1920s. Such books included Austin Whittlesey's *Minor Ecclesiastical, Domestic and Garden Architecture of Southern Spain*, 1917, with a preface by architect Bertram Goodhue; antiques dealers Arthur and Mildred Byne's many books, including *Spanish Architecture of the Sixteenth Century*, 1917, *Spanish Gardens and Patios*, 1924, and *Majorcan Houses and Gardens*, 1928.

Antiques dealers, architects and designers gained skilled familiarity with the Spanish periods, using stylistic labels and dates that associated them to traditional western European periods, such as those used by British historian Sir Banister Fletcher in his *History of Architecture*: the Islamic/Gothic period from the twelfth to sixteenth centuries; the Renaissance/*Plateresco* period with *Mudéjar* decorative details from 1492 to 1556; the Classical/*Desornamentado* period from 1556 to 1650; the Baroque/*Churrigueresco* period from 1650-1750; and the Late Baroque-Rococo period with influence from France and Italy, from 1750 to 1800.

SPAIN'S ISLAMIC/GOTHIC PERIOD, 12TH — 16TH CENTURIES

Spain has a long history of Islamic architecture and decorative arts, and the term "Islamic" is interchanged with the terms Moslem, Saracenic and Moorish, depending on which Arabic group impacted Spain at the time. The European country had been a part of the Grand Roman Empire, and in the medieval centuries it was Christian but overtaken in great part by Moslems so that by late fifteenth century, in different kingdoms, Spain was run variously by Christian kings and Moslem rulers. The Spanish Inquisition of 1477 was intended to unify the Christian country and eliminate Moslems and Jews, but some Islamic control remained until the fall of the Moors at Granada in 1492.

Islamic influence remained a salient aspect of Spanish art and architecture into the late sixteenth century and well beyond that era in terms of crafts, decorative arts and motifs. Spain retained what is commonly referred to as the *Mudéjar* style, a term derived from the Arab word, *mudejalat*, meaning "subdued." Highly skilled artisans, who were Jewish or Moslem, continued to work for the Spaniards, producing furniture, textiles, and architectural ornament with complex repetitive, geometric patterns that appeared "subdued" to the surface of the material whether it was wood, metal, leather, stucco or stone.

Spain's Gothic style developed along French lines and was introduced around 1210. It was primarily applied to church architecture but included the taste for pointed arches and quatrefoil windows on domestic structures as well. The decorations of sculpted and carved classical forms and the painted ornaments and figurative scenes had a naïve, medieval appearance that lasted late into the sixteenth century. However, Spanish architecture also retained its Islamic imprint — producing dense areas of elaborate ornament, maintaining axial organization and courtyards with channeled waterways, and interior wall treatments, lamps and furnishings with elaborate geometric ornament.

The Alhambra in Granada, built and added onto throughout the fourteenth century, was one of the key monuments of this era that was so inspiring to historians and foreign advocates of Spanish style. It was a fortified ruling palace of the Moslem Nasrid dynasty set in gardens, and the restraint of the exterior public walls — opened by very few Gothic double-arched windows — denied the decorative complexity of the interiors and inner courtyards. The principal part of the palace consists of two rectangular courts, one reserved for the use of the sovereign and his entourage, and the other for public ceremonial use. The latter is the Court of the Lions, surrounded by an arcade in which very slender columns with high dosseret blocks carry a perforated arcade structure of pierced and interlaced stucco.

While furnishings were minimal — built-in seating, cushions, tables and free-standing copper braziers — the interior structure presented endless fields of arabesques and filigree detail, niches and tilework. There are halls with domes of stalactite wood-and-stucco detail and vertical surfaces covered with carved stucco. The fragile perforated surfaces often produced the loss of apparent structural integrity creating an ethereal appearance.

The Court of Lions in the Alhambra palace was a public ceremonial space. Pointed arches, slender columns, pierced and interlaced ornament, as well as a central fountain and water channels, are picturesque Arab elements, which were copied in Moorish revival buildings and included in Spanish style works. The intricate craftsmanship of these Arab-inspired decorations rendered in stone, plaster, wood, tile and metal were called *Mudéjar* designs and they continued to appear throughout the various centuries and periods of Spanish design.

One wall of the Alhambra palace at Granada, Spain, shows the essential character of Spain's Islamic/Gothic design of the twelfth through sixteenth centuries. The plane of the wall is emphasized and the few small Gothic-style windows and doors that break the plane are detailed with complex Arabic stucco or stone ornament that is contained within well-defined two- and three-dimensional boundaries.

CALIFORNIA'S SPANISH ISLAMIC/GOTHIC REVIVAL

Rarely was Spain's Islamic/Gothic style copied in entirety in California structures. Victorians of the 1880s and 1890s era better appreciated the exotic style for exposition rooms and the occasional smoking salon, than those from the Spanish Revival period of the 1920s. Nonetheless, the Zwebells used it for their Patio del Moro courtyard apartments, and Glendale's city father Leslie C. Brand employed the style for his elaborate 1902-04 "El Miradero" estate.

Even the leading Spanish Colonial Revival architect, George Washington Smith, attempted a version of the Islamic for an architectural folly, a 1927 natatorium for the beach house of Albert Isham, near Montecito. The indoor pool with changing rooms, included a seating area before a large European-style fireplace — uncommion to

Arab sources were used in the Zwebells' design of the Patio del Moro Apartments. The Moorish style was the request of their client who had traveled to North Africa and Spain. The planar treatment of the wall, a horseshoe arch, *Mudéjar*-like garage door paneling and exotic metal balconies are Arab-Moorish details that are often a part of Spanish Revival designs.

Pointed arches, quatrefoil ornament and minaret-like towers of the Moorish style were introduced by architect Nathaniel Dryden for Leslie C. Brand's 1902-1904 estate in Glendale. Although it was said to be inspired by an East Indian pavilion at the 1893 World's Columbian Exposition, Chicago, the formal elements and the Spanish name "El Miradero," "The Look Out Point," express its Spanish-Moorish influence.

Spain's Islamic/Gothic buildings that were warmed with braziers. The exterior was reserved with pointed arched openings, a dome, minaret and a fortress-like crenellated roofline. Inside, there were *Mudéjar*-style wood doors, metal hardware, hanging copper-and-glass lanterns, and broad wood cornices surrounding the pool area's retractable roof. Also, the Islamic horseshoe arches, columns and entire walls of the interior were covered with Arabic-style tilework.

Another more restrained example was by Addison Mizner, Florida's leading Spanish Colonial Revival architect. He preferred the exotic aspects of the Spanish Islamic/Gothic style and he came to Santa Barbara in the late 1920s to design such a house. Called Casa Bienvenida, 1930, the stone and stucco house features double pointed arch windows, Gothic pointed arch entrances and an ornate cornice along the roofline. On one terrace with chain-laced spiral balusters, an Islamic/

Gothic fountain is the central focus. Mizner preferred to use the Gothic/Islamic style for its stylistic variety of classical forms to interact with the classical Italianate elements of the gardens planned by landscaper Lockwood de Forest and based on the gardens of the eighteenth-century Villa Lante.

More common was the decorative use of Islamic/Gothic details in Spanish Andalusian styled works. Stiles Clements, design partner with Morgan, Walls and Clements, used many of the style's details in the design of the Adamson House, 1928, in Malibu. The entrance facade includes a Gothic stair tower and bottle-glass windows. The opposite facade facing a cove and ocean view has a central patio flanked by side wings which are flat-roofed, one-story Islamic-styled pavilions sheathed in tiles and opened with large Islamic pointed arch windows.

Clements designed the house for Meritt Huntley Adamson and his wife Rhoda Rindge Adamson, who was from an early California founding family. The Rindge family owned Malibu Potteries and produced the tiles for the house. Throughout the structure and the gardens are Spanish-Islamic tilework for fountains, floors, bathrooms and kitchen counters. Tiles cover door and window facings, window jambs and seats, stair risers, and fountains.

The Spanish Islamic/Gothic style also worked well for the 1920s trend for exotic commercial structures. Talented architect Roland E. Coate designed a Calpet gas station in 1928 in the style for a client who had also commissioned an Andalusian-style home. The tiny one-story structure appeared quite grand with its multi-colored tiled dome and tiled wainscoting. At its opening, Moorish-costumed attendants manned the pumps.

Many flat roof Moorish structures had fortress-like crenelations and another Moorish-inspired detail at the Adamson House is the chevron pattern of the pavilion roofline.

Often Moorish elements or details were added to Spanish Andalusian houses as at the Adamson House in Malibu, 1928, designed by Stiles Clements. It includes Moorish style brick chimney pots, pointed arch windows, tile wall surfacing, and flat roof pavilions for the living and dining rooms.

SPAIN'S RENAISSANCE/*PLATERESCO* STYLE, 1492-1556

Clearly defined dates bracket Spain's Renaissance/*Plateresco* Period. It begins in 1492 with the fall of Granada and Christopher Columbus's discovery of America, and it ends with the commencement of Phillip II's reign. "*Plateresco*" comes from the word *plateria* that means silverwork. Silverworking forms, such as a pilaster paneled with arabesques or the tapered candelabrum shaft, were applied to buildings by Spanish architects. The minuteness and fineness of the Renaissance/*Plateresco* ornament in architecture was similar to the decorative detail of the Spanish silverwork that was in greater supply since discovering an abundance of the metal in the New World.

The *Plateresco* style had fundamental Gothic elements that carried on into the mid-sixteenth century with the exuberant production of the *Mudéjar* crafts as well as including Renaissance or "new" elements of an Italian influence. The origins for the decorative style were from early sixteenth-century Italian sculptors and artisans who came to Spain to execute commissions for tombs and altars for Spanish nobles and church officials. This period produced a defined style as rich as any that could be found in other European countries.

"Arcuated" Spanish architecture has come to be widely known in North America from the mission arcades. However, Spanish architecture and its most common vernacular forms were primarily of post-and-lintel, or "trabeated," construction. Arches did come into more common usage in Spain after the Italian Renaissance influence, and it was only later in the sixteenth century that Spanish houses introduced vaulted architecture and a type of studied architectural movement that impacted domestic works.

The Renaissance/*Plateresco* style had a classical Renaissance framework, delineating its outlines and silhouettes; nonetheless, within its classical contours, the style was a highly decorative one reflecting its strong *Mudéjar* craft influence. It regularly included dadoes of polychrome tiles, called *azulejos*, and door and window openings framed with flat bands of patterned plasterwork, called *yeseria*, along with cornices and wide moldings of decorative carved woodwork, called *artesonada*. Interiors could also include sumptuous tapestries and gilded leather hangings and panels.

Seville retained strong *Mudéjar* traditions after 1492, and the Duke of Alba's Palace located in that city was built during the late fifteenth century with sixteenth-century additions. It was an amplification of an Arab house — a courtyard house with multiple patios and Renaissance-style columns, capitals and arched openings. Customary to the Spanish house, one side of a courtyard patio was left open at the second-story level to form a terrace overlooking the garden.

While the courtyards appear at first glance like those of an Italian Renaissance palazzo, in the palace's main patio, the Renaissance marble columns are supported by richly worked *Mudéjar yeseria* arches and door frames. The doors to the interiors are huge *Mudéjar* wooden ones that are swung on pivots like those used in the Alhambra, where the lower pivot is sunken into the floor and the upper one is held by a project-

The Duke of Alba's Palace, Seville, late fifteenth to early sixteenth centuries, is representative of the Spanish Renaissance/*Plateresco* style which began in 1492 with the fall of the Moors at Granada and ended when Phillip II came to power in 1556. One of its courtyards shows classical Italian Renaissance influence on the moldings of the structure but the elongation of the upper portions of the arches shows the formal influence of Moorish horseshoe arches.

ing corbel.

The palace includes wooden Islamic *mushrabiyah*, or boxed-in windows, and a Gothic stone parapet, and inside, one of the main rooms features a wooden beamed ceiling resting on a luxurious *yeseria* frieze about three feet high. The ceiling beams are interspersed with decorated panels that appear practically black, having foliate ornament dramatically picked out in red, light blue and gold. Throughout, the metalwork hanging lamps are *Mudéjar* in shape and execution.

Another Renaissance/*Plateresco* house, which many Americans of the 1920s could have seen on tours and illustrated in English language books and guidebooks, was the early sixteenth century house in Toledo of the painter Domenikos Theolokopoulos, called El Greco. It was designed by Enrique de Egas, who was active from approximately 1480 to 1534. It's clear that Egas adopted some Renaissance elements that he likely derived out of classic details in Gothic designs, rather than seeing Italian Renaissance works firsthand. The house included a terrace overlooking the garden, and the interior courtyard had the traditional trabeated form with wooden columns and bracket capitals. Colorful *azulejos* surrounded the courtyard walls and finish off the walls and a built-in seat in the working area of the kitchen. Toledo, like Seville, was another *Mudéjar* city that remained a formal stronghold after the Moors were expelled, and the house's tilework, decorative stucco door frames, wood cornices and bracket columns expressed the ornate *Mudéjar* crafts.

CALIFORNIA'S SPANISH RENAISSANCE/*PLATERESCO* REVIVAL

In California, the ornamented *Plateresco* style was frequently intermixed with other Spanish Revival styles but was seen occasionally in a nearly pure form on some formal public buildings and some grand houses. One such work is the *Plateresco*-influenced San Diego Museum of Art, built for the 1915 exposition by William Templeton Johnson. Above the museum's ornate entryway are the coats of arms of San Diego, California, Spain and America, and full statues of Spanish painters Murillo, Zurburan and Velazquez. The facade shows the silverwork style with attached columns appearing like delicate filigree.

Among *Plateresco* residences, there is the James Degnan House, 1927, located in La Cañada-Flintridge and designed by Paul Williams, who had a prestigious fifty-

Top to bottom

A *Plateresco* style door at the Duke of Alba's Palace shows how the decorative Moorish *Mudéjar* tradition adopted *plateria*, or silverwork, forms for decorative architectural detail. Well-defined borders contain the architectural stucco, stonework or plasterwork, called *yeseria*, to panels, which surround windows and doors like this one. As here, decorative forms during this period were frequently based on classical Renaissance examples, however, they would be interspersed with other designs that retained the interlace geometric patterns of the *Mudéjar* tradition.

In the Duke of Alba's Palace, a painted and carved beamed ceiling is an example of *Plateresco artesonada*, or woodwork. Also, the broad *yeseria* ceiling cornice and bronze Moorish chandelier show how strongly Moorish *Mudéjar* craftsmanship continued into Spain's Renaissance/*Plateresco* period.

In Toledo, the early sixteenth century house of the painter El Greco, Domenikos Theotokopoulos, displayed the *Plateresco* style of a provincial home. The courtyard featured a doorway surrounded with *Plateresco yeseria*. Bands of tiles, or *azulejos*, formed a dado and decorated the stair risers. The balcony opened the upper rooms to the courtyard.

Located in La Cañada-Flintridge, Califor-nia, the Degnan Residence, 1927, by Paul Williams is a rare example of the revival of the regal Spanish Renaissance/*Plateresco* style. The entrance door clearly shows the "silverwork" style with its finials and tapered columns that resemble elements that might be from a Spanish candelabra. The door surround exhibits Renaissance decorations and a classical shell motif.

eight-year career in Los Angeles, producing many fine period style designs. His entrance for the residence appears like a typical Spanish *Plateresco* design borrowed from one of the Spanish Revival copy books. The *Mudéjar* "silversmith" technique appears around the ornate entrance doorway with exuberant stucco and stone ornament, tall finials and projecting semi-circular balcony. The pierced window openings and elaborate wrought-iron window grills on the entrance facade also display Williams' deft handling of the *Mudéjar* crafts of the Spanish Renaissance/*Plateresco* style.

The terrace facades opening to the ballroom and living room are more typical Renaissance characteristics, as well as the arched loggias, ornate half-columns and Italianate della Robia-like sculpted terra cotta relief panels. Williams also used the common Renaissance-period geometries in the planning: a cubic volume defines at least two rooms, the prestigious 25-by-25-foot stair hall and the smaller study.

Another Southern California residence displaying the *Plateresco* style is the Casa de las Campanas, 1926, located in Hancock Park, by architect Lester Scherer. Lucile Mead, the daughter of Willis Howard Mead, one of the owners of a leading Los Angeles lumber company, Whiting Mead, had input into the design, showing the impact of travel and study on the clients as well as the designers. The house is a two-story structure, which incorporates a low stair tower at the front and, at the rear, a triple-story clock-and-bell tower; the house and side wings surround a rear courtyard. Although the house has Andalusian farmhouse aspects, its Renaissance/*Plateresco* decorative elements are strong.

Piecemeal details from the Spanish Renaissance/ *Plateresco* movement were adopted in California for vernacular Spanish houses. The Casa de las Campanas, 1926, in Los Angeles, featured a *Plateresco* entrance door. Note the well-defined decorative stone surround, contained in both two- and three-dimensions. The ornament includes *Mudéjar* interlace patterns along the inner border.

Accenting the facade is a *Mudéjar*-styled carved wood balcony and a wood detailed, faceted-glass bay window, and most particularly, the *yeseria*-style intricate detailing of the creamy limestone entrance door surround. These wood and stone carvings, as well as the patterned-wood entrance door and hanging incense burner-type metal lamps, betray the *Mudéjar* elements intertwined in the California 1920s Spanish Revival design.

The *Plateresco* style worked well for creating dramatic entrance doors and window treatments for a number of low-rise office buildings and shops in the mid-Wilshire area of Los Angeles. Such formality of style worked well for applying to offices and apartment dwellings and well-organized mixed-use buildings. Several were the works of the firm of Morgan, Walls and Clements, such as the late 1920s Carondelet-Wilshire complex which included a theater, restaurant and offices. Another of the firm's work was the Chapman Park Market and Studios, 1928-29, a two-block project that allowed for parking courtyards hidden by the front street-oriented buildings. Corner towers are articulated in the *Plateresco* ornament where the two greyish-stone buildings separate to accommodate the side street and capitalize on the corner locations. At the street level, the two buildings accommodate stores and offices and are ornamented profusely around their doors and windows. In terms of planning, one of the blocks has ingeniously organized studios/apartments on the second level, where a corridor provides an interior street with double-height skylit studios on one side and double-story apartments on the other.

In Los Angeles, the revival of the Spanish *Plateresco* style created dramatic entrance doors and windows for a number of office buildings and shops. Morgan, Walls and Clements designed several multi-use projects in the style, including the late 1920s Carondelet-Wilshire complex. In addition to the stonework of the side entrance door, the pierced walls, plasterwork and dense grillwork are appropriate to the style.

Casa de Las Campanas was also given a wood *Plateresco* style entrance door carried out in a 1926 version of Spanish *artesonado* craftsmanship. The interlace geometric pattern and the incense-burner type hanging lamp are typical Moorish *Mudéjar* forms.

Spain's Classical/*Desornamentado* Style, 1556-1650

In sixteenth century Spain, the ascetic taste of Philip II was responsible for a close adherence to Italian Renaissance art. The movement took shape under the influence of peripatetic sculptors and architects who were Italian or trained in the style of the Italian Renaissance. However, it was particularly because of Juan de Herrera, who had visited both Flanders (1547-51) and Italy (1551-59) and had become a pupil of Michelangelo, that the Spanish style took a more austere turn. Herrera's reserved style, firmly based in the undecorated classical forms, gave cause for the term *Desornamentado*.

Herrera completed the palatial El Escorial, in Madrid, 1559-84, in this style for Philip II, although it was begun earlier by Juan Batista de Toledo. The final structure was an austere group of Doric Order classical buildings that included four compounds, one each for a monastery, college, church and palace. The geometric grid plan divided the compound into quarters and each compound was divided further, such as the monastery quarter with four square internal courts, each surrounded with three-story arcades.

El Escorial's four lengthy external facades were five-stories high and made from great blocks of granite. The grand central entrance on the west facade opened into the "Patio de los Reyes" lying between the great courts of the monastery and the college, which formed the atrium of the church.

The facade of the church was based on the High Renaissance church of S. Maria di Carignano in Genoa by Peruzzi, and was built of yellowish-gray granite, a hard material that markedly restrained the architect. Generally devoid of ornament, the entire Doric Order compound was remarkably dignified with plain facades and towers, the whole group culminating in the great western towers and central dome of the church.

While the *Desornamentado* style influenced some Spanish buildings and Spanish colonial structures, it lasted less than one hundred years and was generally accompanied by the continuing Gothic and *Plateresco* elements, which better expressed the vitality and colorful nature of Spanish design and decoration.

In Spain, the reign of Phillip II, beginning in 1556, signaled a move toward classical design. This movement lasted almost a hundred years and the best known example is Phillip's palace compound, called El Escorial, which included a monastery, college and church. The simplest classical order, the Doric, was employed and little ornament was included other than the classical moldings, giving rise to the name *Desornamentado* for the movement.

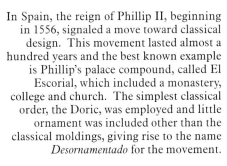

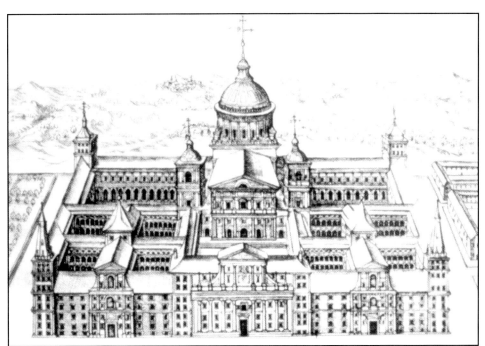

CALIFORNIA'S SPANISH CLASSICAL REVIVAL: MEDITERRANEAN STYLE

Some of California's imported altarpieces and mission facades were influenced by the classicism of Spain's sixteenth- to seventeenth-century *Desornamentado* movement. However, a 1920s period style revivalist would likely work in the Italianate mode, not Spanish classical, if his or her client's taste was for the classical style. Most frequently, the style required working in stone rather than the stucco and adobe associated with the missions and typical Spanish casas.

Spanish picture books and Beaux Arts architectural educations offered revivalists the opportunity to copy highly classical elements from the El Escorial and justify that they were still working in the Spanish style. In addition, some classical stone Italianate buildings seemed to get a Spanish reputation purely by association with the Southern California setting — like the classical, domed Pasadena City Hall, 1925-27, by Bakewell and Brown.

There are no pure Spanish *Desornamentado* revival buildings in California, although there are many referred to as "Mediterranean" style and are highly classical Spanish, like the Pasadena City Hall, mentioned above, and the Southern California Automobile Club, 1921-23, Los Angeles, with its greyish stonework, tall arches and internal courtyard, by Hunt and Burns, and Roland Coate.

The term Mediterranean encompasses many cultures — from the southern portions of Spain, France and Greece, the Spanish islands, Moorish North Africa and the coasts of Italy — but the Spanish and Italianate styles were the most influential to the California Mediterranean. Both styles had terraces, courtyards, tile roofs, window grills, carved wood doors and painted ceilings. Italianate structures could have reserved stone mouldings, capitals, columns and cornices, while Spanish ones tended to use more robust carved and sculpted ornament and colorful tile walls and paving.

The courtyard arcade of a 1920s Los Angeles house by Gordon Kaufmann expresses the simple elegance of *Desornamentado* classicism with slender columns and delicate Corinthian capitals. The *corredor* is paved in tile accented with decorative pavers, and, along with the tile wall fountain, hanging lantern and wrought iron grill door, the decoration shows Spanish influence on an otherwise Italian Renaissance design.

From late 1928 through 1929, California architects associated with the American Institute of Architects decided that there was a new style particular to Southern California, variously referred to as Spanish and Mediterranean, and felt it could be called "California style" since it was so popular in the state. Whenever the stylistic forms appear somewhat Spanish and somewhat Italian — a hybrid of the two cultures — the style is usually considered Mediterranean. It's similar to the Spanish Classical *Desornamentado* with a more relaxed California plan, due to the scale of the rooms, the wide *portales*, or *corredors*, and spacious terraces, as well as slightly more ornamental detail, due to the use of California-made tiles, grillwork, painted ceilings, and carved and modeled ornamental detail.

Expressions of the classical reserve of the *Desornamentado* style were present in the restrained entrance facades of Andalusian-style houses. Similar facades were created by Southern California's leaders of the Spanish Revival: the Vinmont House, 1926, in Los Feliz, by Roland Coate; the Bradbury House, 1922, in Santa Monica, by John Byers; the Helms House, 1928-33, in Beverly Hills, by Gordon Kaufmann; the Hebenton House, 1916, in Santa Barbara, by George Washington Smith; and the Osthoff House, 1924, in San Marino, also by Smith.

Other Mediterranean Spanish Revival houses tended to express horizontality and a close relationship to nature, such as another Gordon Kaufmann house, the Cottrell Residence, circa 1926, in Hancock Park. Just inside the austere, rectangular block entrance, the design featured an open-air atrium. It had a strong sense of exterior and interior living, with rooms that opened in various ways and various heights to an

The front elevation of the Osthoff House, 1924, San Marino, by George Washington Smith, is one of many reserved facades which appeared similar to a number of Spanish Revival homes, including John Byers' Bradbury House, Santa Monica, 1922, and Roland Coate's Vinmont House, 1926, Los Angeles. It shows design restraint and simple classical moldings — two characteristics that California's designers derived from classical variations on the Spanish *Desornamentado* style. Despite the reserved exterior, like Andalusian farmhouses, the courtyards and interiors of these revival houses included Spanish woodwork, metalwork and tiles that continued to emulate decorative *Mudéjar* traditions.

internal courtyard. Likewise, Wallace Neff's Haldeman House, 1939, in Beverly Hills, also emphasized the horizontality of the structure. At the entrance, the two-story house was flush to the ground of a grass forecourt, originally decorated with classical urns. The low pitch of the tile roof also highlighted the horizontal character and terraces — located above the entrance and at the sides and back — were snuggly related to the roofline, making the house appear a very modern composition of light walls and deep, shadowed terraces. Neff also added another Mediterranean form, likely borrowed from the Balearic islands. It was the window shutter tipped up from the bottom in a manner that covered each window and appeared reserved and enclosed, yet relaxed and tropical.

Another Neff design, the 1926 Niblo Residence, could be called a Mediterranean house. It was most unusual for its circular plan forming a grand enclosed motor court, and the rear facade with its arched loggia like a mission *portal*. The circular court and the classical treatment of the rear loggia reflect Neff's notion of Roman classical buildings and perhaps the circular influence from the plan of Nero's first century Golden Palace in Rome on the otherwise Spanish design.

A dignified wood, glass, and metal door of the 1920s Gordon Kaufmann design opens to the central courtyard. The stone surround reveals the same sober classicism as found at Spain's El Escorial.

Spain's Baroque/*Churrigueresco* Style, 1650-1750

Spain's Baroque period, circa 1650-1750, occurred when its culture was thoroughly entrenched in the Spanish universities located in Mexico and South America, and it produced many fine buildings throughout the Spanish colonies. The style is characterized by a reaction from the rigid formalism of Herrera and his followers, displaying an extraordinary exuberance, opulence and fluid exaggeration of classical forms. The extravagant style is known as *Churrigueresco* because it is based on the late seventeenth-century work of Jose de Churriguera (1650-1723), although he was not the most extreme exponent of the style.

Like Gianlorenzo Bernini's work in Italy during the Counter Reformation, *Churrigueresco* religious work heightened spiritual fervor, fusing painting and sculpture into a form of architecture which seemed to break out of its structural bounds. Similar to Bernini's mid-seventeenth century Cornaro Chapel in Rome, the Transparente Chapel in the Toledo Cathedral is exceptionally dramatic. The *Churrigueresco* work was completed in 1732 by Narcisco Tomé, one of the most brilliant followers of the style, active between 1715 and 1742. Tomé's work was mainly sculptural; however, the Transparente Chapel is a theatrical example adding painting and sculpture with optical illusions and dazzling illumination of religious figures and scenes.

The *Churrigueresco* style also worked well for grand palaces and public buildings, such as the Provincial Hospital in Madrid, designed by Pedro Ribera and begun in 1722, and the Dos Aguas Palace in Valencia. The palace's sculptural decoration was done by Ignacio Vergara in 1740-44 and it concentrated upon the entrance portal where a sculpture of the Virgin Mary above the door is in a cabinet that can be opened or closed. Beside the entrance doors are twisting allegorical figures that were inspired by Michelangelo's early sixttenth-century Medici tomb figures in Florence.

Like Spain's *Plateresco* style, *Churrigueresco* ornament tended to focus around the doors and window of a structure. However, at the mid-eighteenth century Dos Aguas Palace in Valencia, Spain, the facade is opened with many windows, and the lively stone and stucco decoration tends to spread across the entire facade.

The entrance portal of the Dos Aguas Palace features the elaborate sculpture of Ignacio Vergara from 1740-44. Above the entrance is a statue of the Virgin Mary in a cabinet that can be opened or closed. Flanking the entrance doors are writhing allegorical figures inspired by Michelangelo's early sixteenth-century Medici tombs in Florence.

With an impressive facade that appears like a church. the Provincial Hospital in Madrid, 1722+, was designed by Pedro Ribera. It is designed in Spain's *Churrigueresco* style, which appeared circa 1650 to 1750 and was concurrent with the Spanish settlement of Mexico. The style was characterized by robust Baroque ornament that tended to burst out of clear architectural outlines, as Ribera's entrance door shows. In a *Churrigueresco* structure, the distinction between an architectural framework — like molding borders, niches, window oculi, columns and gable pediments — and its decoration is reduced by its confusion with the proliferate sculptural ornament

California's version of the *Churrigueresco* style never reached the exuberance of the original Spanish works. In fact, when comparing Goodhue and Winslow's entrance buildings for San Diego's 1915 Panama-California Exposition to the *Churrigueresco* works sited in Madrid and Valencia, the California work show the decorative aspects of *Plateresco* design. Ornament is generally confined to an architectural framework and the sculpted and carved shapes appear like finials, tapered columns and lively classical motifs found in Spain's Baroque *plateria*, or silverwork.

California's Spanish Baroque/*Churrigueresco* Revival

California's revival designers intermixed the palatial, ornamented *Plateresco* and *Churrigueresco* styles. In fact, it has become difficult to tell whether an ornate-styled Spanish building is based on *Plateresco* or *Churrigueresco* sources, so restrained are the *Churrigueresco* examples when compared to the robust — almost Rococo — forms of the Transparente and other original Spanish examples. Whether a design was *Plateresco* or *Churrigueresco* was a matter of degree of ornamentation, or whether the design was copied from a Spanish design of a particular date — *Plateresco* works from the sixteenth century and *Churrigueresco* works from the eighteenth century.

These styles worked best on towers and larger public buildings, as used on the Hollywood Chamber of Commerce Building, by Morgan, Walls and Clements, 1925; and the Beverly Hills City Hall, 1931, by William Gage and Robert Korner; and, as mentioned above, on the California Building by Bertram Goodhue and Carleton Winslow at San Diego's 1915 Panama-California Exposition. As the official entrance to the fair, the California Tower soared up two hundred feet and was topped with a blue-and-white tile dome. The thick sculptural ornament was primarily organized around the doorway and windows, adhering to the manner of the *Plateresco yeseria*, while the remainder of the wall was smooth and generally unadorned.

A principal Southern California landmark of the *Churrigueresco* style is the Church of St. Vincent de Paul, in Los Angeles, 1923-25, by the firm of Albert C. Martin. It was based on the Church of Santa Prisa, a *Churrigueresco* church in Taxco, Mexico, seen by Edward and Carrie Estelle Doheny, chief donors to the project. Features of

In Los Angeles, Saint Vincent's Church, 1923-25, by the firm of Albert C. Martin, was copied after Santa Prisa, a Mexican *Churrigueresco* style church in Taxco. In Mexico as in California, the *Churrigueresco* style is often hard to distinguish from subdued versions of the *Plateresco* style, as the Church displays the same *plateria* aspects as the San Diego fair buildings. Nonetheless, the Church's stone ornament is a bit more three-dimensional and robust than the earlier San Diego example.

the design are a *Churrigueresco*-decorated entrance facade of Indiana limestone and a brilliantly colored tile dome that spans 45 feet. The interior ceiling decoration was by one of the leading ceiling painters of the Revival period styles, John B. Smeraldi, who worked as fluently in the Spanish styles as he did in the Italian.

Carleton Winslow settled in California after designing the 1915 San Diego Exposition buildings with Goodhue, and had the opportunity to apply the elaborate *Churrigueresco* style to the design of a single-family residence for a wealthy client. His 1918 Bliss House in Montecito (now Casa Dorinda, a retirement home) includes palatial massing and elaborate *Churrigueresco* stone-and-stucco ornament around the doors and windows.

On the Coronado peninsula near San Diego, Elmer Grey designed the *Churrigueresco* style Rew-Sharp House, in 1918, following the recent San Diego fair. With the small entrance "plaza" and the prestigious carved stone entrance, the small scale stucco house was given a dramatic appearance that is still well-maintained and inspiring to this day.

However, the most elaborate *Churrigueresco*-influenced residence was Julia Morgan's grandiose William Randolph Hearst residence, called San Simeon, 1919-47. Also known as Hearst Castle, the church-like facade of the main residence, called Casa Grande, was based on the church of Santa Maria la Mayor in Ronda, Spain, built during the fourteenth through sixteenth centuries. While the facade is based on a *Plateresco*-period church, Morgan made it more ornate to be considered a *Churrigueresco* design, and in many ways the Baroque-styled terraces, Roman Pool and magnificence of the entire estate pays tribute to the grandiose, larger-than-life *Churrigueresco* style. The estate includes enormous grounds and three large guest houses located at the hilltop site — the highest promontory of the central California acreage, which overlooks the Pacific. The estate also includes an indoor pool, and once maintained a zoo.

The houses of the estate mimic other Spanish, Moorish, English and French period style details as well, with imported elements from all of these cultures and spanning periods from medieval to Baroque. In the Casa Grande, Morgan managed to incorporate many imported Spanish ceilings as well as other imported architectural fragments. The refectory (dining room) has a coffered ceiling and side paneling of fifteenth-century Spanish choir stalls, and the billiard room has a fifteenth-century Spanish ceiling and sixteenth- to eighteenth-century Persian tile panels and spandrels. A Spanish-Moorish ceiling is featured in the library, and the north Gothic bedroom has a fifteenth-century ceiling from a Cordovan castle. The interiors feel appropriate to the urbane Spanish *Churrigueresco* era, during which a palace might include many elements from European travel and influence. It includes Spanish imports and furnishings from many periods. However, the project is important for the many California Spanish Revival furnishings and building crafts made specifically for the house by the team of craftspersons who worked with Morgan on this long-term Hearst commission.

The *Churrigueresco* style was a major style in Mexico and many of its buildings — like the Taxco church which inspired the St. Vincent's Church, mentioned above — were copied throughout Southern California. The general form of Mexican *Churrigueresco* works, however, tended to simplify and exaggerate the bold baroque shapes in a manner that appeared Mayan and Aztecan in execution. An example of

The Rew-Sharp House, 1918, located on the Coronado peninsula near San Diego was a rare example of the monumental *Churrigueresco* style applied to a suburban home. Pasadena architect Elmer Grey designed the house shortly after the San Diego fair, giving the small entrance the feeling of a "plaza" and applying ornate stone carving to the door surround as well as to the quatrefoil-shaped fountain with its elaborate tiered basins.

The *Churrigueresco* style worked well for low-rise offices and public buildings such as the East Los Angeles Union Pacific Railroad Passenger Station, 1928, by Gilbert Stanley Underwood. The station was designed in a Mexican version of the *Churrigueresco* style with cast stone ornament and heavy ironwork grills. When compared to its Spanish prototypes, Mexican *Churrigueresco* works simplified and exaggerated the robust baroque shapes in a manner that appeared Mayan and Aztecan in execution.

Centuries of vernacular works from Spain's provinces, particularly Andalusia, inspired the greatest number of Southern California's Spanish Revival designs due to their publication in America by architects, scholars and connoisseurs of Spanish art, architecture and decorative arts. Such images as this plain farmhouse from the early twentieth century, located near Valencia, Spain, inspired the restrained, flat planar character of some revival works.

Another plain looking Andalusian hacienda from the late nineteenth century shows that the appearance of Spain's long, low tile-roofed courtyard houses were in many ways similar to California's early adobes.

this tendency can be seen in the remains of the East Los Angeles Union Pacific Railroad Passenger Station, 1928, by Gilbert Stanley Underwood, characterized by cast stone ornament and heavy ironwork grills.

Spanish Provincial: Andalusian Vernacular, 12th — 19th Centuries

For North Americans and especially Southern Californians, the most influential Spanish structures are the provincial vernacular building forms, particularly southern Spain's Andalusian farmhouses, haciendas and casas. These buildings were of no particular influence and not especially worthy of study for the Spanish, South Americans or Mexicans. But in North America, the images of these common buildings became the cause for a Spanish Revival style both for public and private work. Sketches and photographs of these structures, their details and gardens were published in the books by Mildred and Arthur Byne, such as their *Provincial Houses in Spain*, 1927, and many other titles, such as *Spanish Farm Houses and Minor Public Buildings*, 1924, by Winsor Soule with an introduction by a respected architect, Ralph Adams Cram. Texts were brief, but these picture books illustrated examples of all sorts of common buildings and decorative details that could be easily and reasonably adapted or seen on future travels to the cities of Seville, Granada, Cordova and Valencia, and smaller towns and villages like Avila, Jaen and Cacerres.

City halls, jails, bull-rings, bath houses and other public buildings in out-of-the-way locations provided structure and detail to copy. However, the Spanish *cortijo* farm was most influential, and there were many illustrations of the haciendas and farm-houses with walled pass-throughs or large wooden gates leading to the *cortijo* or courtyard. Farms also had various types of towers and unusual angled walls.

Wooden balconies in the carved and faceted *Mudéjar* style could be copied from the houses and small public buildings, and the books presented page after page of various styles for window grills. There were also gardens with parterres and fountains, and garden walls from farmhouses and city houses; and scalloped walls like those from the Plaza de Toros at Ronda.

Wrought iron grills were a necessity for any Spanish Revival work and Spanish picture books were virtual catalogs providing designers and architects with ideas for their shape and construction.

Provincial areas maintained the greatest *Mudéjar* influence, and retained medieval ways of building and a respect for common, simple furnishings. In these locales, the character and essence of the Spanish culture could be tangibly experienced, and the greatest number of the books' images came from the provinces, particularly Andalusia, in the southern portion of the country, where the influence of the Arabic cultures remained strong.

CALIFORNIA'S SPANISH PROVINCIAL ANDALUSIAN STYLE

"In California, the original borrowing was Spanish. . . . California houses were as nearly like the houses of Andalusia as the crudity of materials and the dearth of workmen could make them. For it was the Spanish province of Andalusia which sent the first soldiers and adventurers to California...."
— Roland Coate, "The Early California House; Blending Colonial and California Forms," March, 1929, *California Arts and Architecture.*

Revivalists usually enjoy improving on their original source, and the Spanish Provincial style provided the framework for freely applying any and all Spanish elements and ornament — Islamic, *Plateresco*, Classical and *Churrigueresco*. In fact, French, English and local Monterey elements could be attached to the framework as well, since individuality and uniqueness was encouraged by the provincial style. In the many Spanish copy books, the everyday components of the provincial styles were presented: reserved exteriors with decorated interiors, asymmetrical compositions with additive elements, courtyards at one or several places — at entrances, sides or backs of the structures. Balconies, grillwork for windows and doors, tile roofs, tile paving and tile decoration were also included.

American architects could use images like this one — the scalloped wall of the Plaza de Toros, at Ronda, circa 1920 — from picture books of Spanish architecture to design common walls and decorative detail for their Spanish Revival works.

Architects in California quickly adopted vernacular Spanish elements and George Washington Smith, who practiced in Santa Barbara, designed the front courtyard facade of the Casa del Herrero, 1922-25, in a casual asymmetrical manner, as if the house had been added to over years. Here, the clients George and Carrie Steedman imported the wood door, stone surround and many of the grills from Spain.

In an ironic, but common, cultural transformation, the revival of Spanish *vernacular* design became an *elitist high style* in domestic architecture on foreign American soil. One particular provincial form frequently copied was the Andalusian farmhouse, a vernacular building type that was skillfully carried out in Southern California by its leader of the Spanish Colonial Revival, George Washington Smith. Smith's designs were romantic and refined, and the strength of his work was that he made ornament subservient to the volume and mass of the structure. Working primarily in Santa Barbara, Smith produced houses that were often L-, H- or U-planned, with surrounding gardens and courtyards laid out on axis with a fountain or pool, pergolas and various terraces or garden rooms.

The best example of his work is likely the Casa del Herrero, 1922-25, located in Montecito. Smith planned the house with its owners, George and Carrie Steedman, to be Andalusian in style, giving the impression of the relaxed symmetries and casual simplicity of a white-walled farmhouse. Open to the public as a house museum, it's now an invaluable local resource for Hispanic decorative arts, as well as a landmark work of Spanish Revival architecture and landscape design.

The kitchen courtyard of the Casa del Herrero features such practical Andalusian farmhouse aspects such as the bell in the niche and the water trough that conducted roof water down to the large rainwater vase, right.

Smith designed the home to be like that of a wealthy Spanish farmer, with the front entrance reached indirectly via a short drive and a courtyard. A tiled fountain punctuates the center of the courtyard, but it isn't aligned with the front door since there is an asymmetrical arrangement of elements of the entrance facade. Iron grills ornament the windows and the entrance is through an antique wood door decorated with a sculpted medieval stone surround.

The Steedmans liked medieval elements, and Lutah Maria Riggs, Smith's talented associate, added an octagonal library off the living room in 1931 based on a French medieval tower. On the opposite side of the house is a formal, central focus: a loggia modeled after the fifteenth-century Villa Cigliano, located in San Casciano in the Pesa River Valley. Although Italian, rather than Spanish in its source, the loggia is in the center of the overall Spanish Andalusian structural block. Both the French library and the Italian loggia show the flexible nature of the Spanish provincial vernacular form to take on piecemeal formal period styles, yet retain its relaxed asymmetry in the total composition. The rear facade looks onto the immense south garden with water channels and pools that are Islamic in form and continue the loggia's centralized axis out into the landscape.

The Steedmans took several trips to Spain, and worked with antiques dealers Mildred and Arthur Byne to buy furniture and architectural elements, as well as commission Tunisian tiles for the house. Throughout the house are antique *Mudéjar* carved wooden doors and window shutters, architectural fragments, chandeliers and sconces, iron grills, leaded windows, garden pots, wrought-iron gates, chairs and tables.

Spanish-Tunisian tiles decorate the kitchen and bathrooms inside the house, as well as the fountains, benches and paving outside, where the planting is often exotic. There is a cactus garden at the far end of the south garden and tropical planting around the entrance courtyard, where the paving is a translation of similar work at the Patio de la Reja at the Alhambra. Landscaping, like the house itself, appears peculiarly Californian yet a masterful work of the eclectic Spanish Revival.

Other architects used the provincial Andalusian style for works in other locations of Southern California, like San Clemente, where the founders, Ole Hanson and Hamilton Cotton, based the town's architecture on the casual style, and architect Virgil Westbrook used it to design many of San Clemente's homes and public buildings.

Carl Lindbom, a Scandinavian immigrant who had a thriving period revival practice in Los Angeles in the 1920s, designed the houses of the town's two founders. He based Cotton's residence, called Casa Pacifica, 1927, on a specific provincial country house in San Sebastian, Spain, which had some delightful small towers. While Lindbom's source was from northern Spain, Cotton thought of the courtyard house as a horseman's hacienda, part of a rancho compound with a thick white wall linking the main house to other buildings around what was roughly a circular-planned, gravel-paved courtyard. Here, hitching posts had been a part of Lindbom's original design. One arched entrance facing this courtyard discloses the inner courtyard of the main house and has been treated as an outdoor living room with a central fountain, a fireplace and an ample paved space for dining. On the other three sides of this outdoor room, large white pillars open to wide, wood-beamed *portales* or *corredors* and to the interior rooms of the house.

Along with Roland Coate, Reginald Johnson, Paul Williams and others, architect Wallace Neff designed some highly picturesque Spanish provincial houses for some of

Wallace Neff's Thomson House, 1923-25, in Beverly Hills, featured an arched passage, which led through the structure to the privacy of the courtyard, similar to the plan of Spanish *cortijo* farmhouses.

the Hollywood set, although Neff's Spanish Revival was merely one style among many in his repertoire. For Frances Marion and Fred Thomson, a film writer and a cowboy actor, respectively, Neff designed an Andalusian farmhouse compound to serve as a California rancho, located on a Beverly Hills hilltop in 1923-25. The compound included a riding ring and an adjoining stable, a house for the ranch hands and the main courtyard house at the top of the ridge.

The entrance drive loops around to the top of the hill and leads to the stone-paved courtyard of the house. The courtyard is reached through a broad pointed-arch passageway located on one wing of the house. The small tunnel passage was a common Andalusian provincial form and one that Neff used on many occasions.

There, at the entrance bay, Neff presents a picturesque "gable chapel" effect that he used again on the entrance bay of other houses and on an earlier church design. The design is likely one which Neff had seen in a Spanish book, since the bay seems to be inspired by *Plateresco* designs. It's articulated on the sides with tapered attached pillars topped with spiraling stone finials.

Crowning the bay is the simple roof gable, and before the arched door of wrought-iron and glass is an arched entrance porch defined by a broad, grey stone surround, set off from the white stucco wall. Like the framing *yeseria* effect of *Plateresco* works, Neff's stone surround is simplified to a minimal spiral motif on the outer edge and a beaded design on the inner edge.

At the Drucker Residence, 1926, in Los Feliz, Neff defined a courtyard entrance with the similar "gable chapel" motif; however, here it's a shallow projecting wing and appears more Italianate in the stone decoration of the door surround. After the residence suffered a fire, Neff remodeled the house in 1934 and turned this rear gable entrance into the main facade. He re-oriented the house inward on the lot, facing what had been the rear courtyard, since it easily suited the manner of an Andalusian farmhouse compound and what he had already established as an important entrance in the 1926 design.

Another Wallace Neff house, the 1926 Drucker House in Los Angeles, presents Andalusian courtyard house aspects, including a gabled chapel motif Neff used at the meeting of two wings to accentuate the west entrance. This entrance originally was considered the rear of the house but when it was remodeled by Neff in 1934, it became the front entrance, emphasizing the importance of the courtyard. Neff's chapel motif was not a new one since many entrances of Spanish farmhouses and palaces in the predominantly Catholic country were articulated in a religious manner and many window grills were crowned with religious crosses.

The east garden facade of Neff's 1926 Drucker house was the original front of the house until Neff remodeled it in 1934. The circular porch minimized the dramatic effect that the three crowning Moorish-style finials have made on the entrance of this restrained, planar Andalusian-style facade.

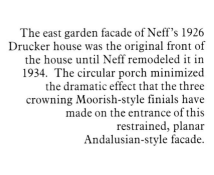

One architect who worked with local Southern California Mexican craftspersons was John Byers, a self-trained architect who had lived briefly in Uruguay and headed the Romance language department at Santa Monica High School from 1910 to 1920. He first became an entrepreneur in his special area of interest — building in the local Mexican adobe tradition. He founded the John Byers Mexican Hand Made Tile Company, hiring local Mexicans to make floor and roof tiles, and his early trademark was adobe construction. However, after the earthquake of 1925 and its effect on building codes, Byers built "adobe-like" structures with floor plans organized around patios and courtyards. He obtained his architect's license in 1926 and opened his new company: John Byers Organization for the Design and Buildng of Latin Houses.

He approached his designs both as a contractor who knew his building craft and as a teacher interested in teaching others about the designs of the Spanish culture. He and his company turned out tiles, weathervanes and other grillwork, door and window hardware, light fixtures, hand-turned wooden balusters, cabinetry, elaborate moldings and wooden brackets for exposed beams of ceilings and courtyard portals.

Along with his partner, Edla Muir, Byers designed Santa Monica's landmark Miles Memorial Playhouse in an Andalusian church form, and he completed numerous Spanish-style houses for clients such as Irving Thalberg and Norma Shearer, Buster Crabbe and J. Paul Getty. He also designed houses for himself and several others on the same tree-lined street, La Mesa Drive, near Pacific Palisades.

In 1926, he completed a modest house in the Spanish-style Palos Verdes community for a development manager, Donald Lawyer. It was immediately considered by the Palos Verdes Art Jury as one of the town's ten most notable buildings. Byers' interest in authenticity was well suited to the Spanish-themed community. The courtyard house — with low garden walls enclosing a garden and pond, and the unobtrusive design of the house and its many Spanish building crafts — represented

Byers' interpretation of a simple provincial house.

In addition to residential design, the provincial Spanish style with its very common elements worked extremely well for some commercial and public structures during the 1920s. One fine example is James Osborne Craig's El Paseo, 1922-24, in Santa Barbara, which provides a great variety of spatial references. There are narrow lanes and open patios with gardens and fountains, and restaurants with mezzanines and lofty triple-height ceilings. Arches and beamed ceilings, awnings and ironwork enhance the experience of shopping, dining and meeting friends and acquaintances in downtown Santa Barbara. There is no major formal, attention-gathering experience of *Plateresco* or *Churrigueresco* high style, just pleasant provincial urban forms as the Spanish model.

Another ingenious work in Spanish provincialism is Franklin Harper's Granada Buildings, 1925, in Los Angeles. It includes four buildings that are conceptually oriented to the public street, a central court and a service court, and the buildings themselves are rational in their use of different Spanish-style doors and windows as playful motifs. The three levels of units are carefully organized into stacked maisonettes, with mezzanines for a mix of uses and creative diversity. The total experience of the buildings is that of an urban fragment with narrow streets and an Old World context. As a monument of Spanish provincial style for the working environment, the Granada Buildings have attracted many talented artists, graphic designers and architects over the years.

CALIFORNIA'S MONTEREY REVIVAL STYLE

"...But when California became a member of the Union and officials, settlers and artisans came to the capital, Monterey, they found Spanish style not to their liking and they added to them details of New England Colonial houses.... Spanish massing, some patios, courts, balconies but [New England-style] double-hung windows, wooden casings, molded trims, entrance doors with side lights and doors of four, six and eight panels."
— Roland Coate, "The Early California House, Blending Colonial and California Forms", March, 1929, *California Arts and Architecture*.

A true Monterey Colonial house was a Spanish-Mexican adobe, usually of two-story height, with double-hung windows and glass-paneled doors, glass transoms, sidelights and fanlights, as well as painted door-, window- and cornice-trim in fluted bands of New England-style wood molding. The house derives from the New England influences in Monterey, California during the 1840s and 1850s, when adobe hacienda construction was masked with painted carpentry details produced by New England shipbuilders who had settled the port town. They added wood floors, wood window and door casements, and would dress up their designs with louvered shutters, picket garden fences, and a running upper balcony that would extend the full length of the facade and likely around several sides of the house.

Balconies are a common building element of *all* Spanish period styles, and there are clear distinctions among those influenced by Spanish period styles, *Mudéjar* crafts and Monterey sources. However, during the Revival 1920s and 30s, so many fine architects added classical wood detail to Spanish-style houses and used balconies in myriad inventive ways that what we call a Monterey Colonial is rarely a pure revival of the style that was created in a local town. Today, most people misjudge a Monterey Colonial revival house as *any* with the most distinguishing element — the ever-common balcony – whether or not it runs the full-length of the facade, whether it is painted white or stained and whether the decorative detail is New England Colonial,

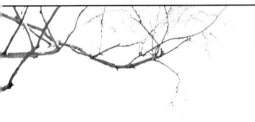

The Spanish Andalusian vernacular was revived for public and commercial work. One example is Franklin Harper's Granada Buildings, 1925, in Los Angeles, which is actually a compound made up of four structures. Different Spanish-style doors and windows are tastefully arranged while the flat, planar character of Andalusian design is maintained along the first two-levels of each building, while the third story steps back to create upper terraces.

Spanish or Moorish.

From Byers to Zwebell, all Spanish Revivalists touched on Monterey Revival elements or produced pure examples of the style. Roland Coate became adept at the style because he felt that both Mediterranean and Monterey Colonial houses were appropriate to the region. Coate had been a partner with Reginald Johnson and Gordon Kaufmann, but opened his own Los Angeles office in 1925, specializing in houses for established clients in Hancock Park, Pasadena and San Marino. His work is appreciated to this day for spacious, airy interiors that open to the outdoors.

One Monterey Revival style house Coate designed for a Hancock Park client — the Fudger House, 1929 — features a balcony that authentically runs along the upper story of the entrance facade. However, the house's richly stained balcony and louvered shutters stand out against the smooth white plaster of the adobe-like house, appearing more exotically *Mudéjar* than Monterey in the color contrast. On the other hand, one of the best and most exacting Monterey Revival designs in Southern California is one by Donald McMurray in Pasadena, 1937. It has a Monterey balcony that runs across the front of the house, along with reserved New England-style moldings and a picket fence that are all painted an American Colonial white in the Monterey fashion.

The Monterey colonial house, developed in the 1830s in Monterey, California is of great importance to the *indigenous* development of the Spanish style in Southern California and its form is relevant to both the Spanish Revival and the Ranch House/Rancho Revival. Although revival works no longer employed adobe construction, one Monterey style house by Donald McMurray in Pasadena, 1937, shows the dominant balcony with simple wood balusters. The balcony, running along the complete front facade, is matched with a picket fence that sets off the first level porch.

CHAPTER THREE

ARCHITECTURAL DETAILS & DECORATIVE ARTS

Inspired architects and their clients in the 1920s and 30s would copy whole Spanish-style facades or tiny bits of decorative detail from an historic example or a beloved building found on a vacation, whether a palace, a church or a simple hacienda. In some Spanish Revival cases, the images and the architectural elements — like doors, window grills or stone door surrounds, tile and furniture — would be imported from Spain, other Mediterranean countries, or Mexico. At other times, they rendered their own contemporary versions of the building crafts and furnishings. In all cases, delightful details and ornament captured both grand and common day-to-day traditions of Spain that had been transported to the idyllic climate and lush landscape of Southern California.

Materials like ceramic tile, brick, stone, concrete, plaster and stucco, metals and wood were articulated by their various methods — carving, incising, painting and forging — to suit the various Spanish styles — Gothic, *Mudéjar*, classical and baroque. During the 1915 to 1940 period, California, the colonial step-child of Spain, was swept up with its Spanish heritage and adhered to it like it was a new-found religion, turning personal spaces into a bit of Spain, with an adopted sense of family pride and an assured sense of timeless elegance.

Representative of some of the best houses by the most talented designers, Spanish Revival architectural and interior design elements included here are from the following residences, from San Diego to San Simeon:

Adamson House, Malibu, 1928, by Stiles Clements of Morgan, Walls & Clements, interior design by John Holtzclaw, now a house museum run by California State Parks

Andalusia Apartments, Hollywood, 1926, by Nina and Arthur Zwebell

Casa de Buena Vista, 1929-35, Montecito, by George Washington Smith and Lutah Maria Riggs, renovated by Margie and Lawrence Schneider

Casa de las Campanas, Los Angeles, 1926, by Lester Scherer and Lucile Mead, renovated by Ann Daniel and Leonard Hill

Casa del Herrero, the residence of George and Carrie Steedman, Montecito, 1922-25, by George Washington Smith, additions by Lutah Maria Riggs, landscape by Ralph T. Stevens and Peter Reidel, now a private house museum

Cottrell Residence, Los Angeles, circa 1926, by Gordon Kaufmann, preserved in the 1990s by designer Jon Cottrell

Degnan Residence, La Cañada-Flintridge, 1926, by Paul Williams, preserved by Gina and Rod Guerra

Drucker Residence, Los Angeles, 1926, remodeled 1934, by Wallace Neff, preserved in the 1990s by Regina and Bruce Drucker

Hearst Castle, the William Randolph Hearst Estate, San Simeon, 1919-1949, by Julia Morgan

Rew-Sharp Residence, Coronado Peninsula, 1919, by Elmer Grey

Thomson Residence, Beverly Hills, 1923-25, by Wallace Neff (demolished)

Also, see the illustrations in Chapter Two for further examples of these residences, as well as illustrations of Spanish sources for the Spanish Revival. Both original Spanish designs and revival works continue to be inspiring.

The central section of the south garden facade of the Casa
del Herrero in Montecito was copied from an Italian
source, a fifteenth-century villa located in San Casciano.
The decorative elements within the volume are, neverthe-
less, Spanish in character or produced from Spanish and
Tunisian imports.

Drawings or photographs of Spanish *Plateresco*
designs likely inspired Paul Williams design of The
Degnan Residence, 1927, La Cañada-Flintridge, now
impeccably restored by its new owners, Rod and
Gina Guerrera.

A Spanish seventeenth-century style wooden door opens the Hearst Castle's morning room to the rear terrace of Casa Grande. It reveals the *Mudéjar* treatment of the design, subduing decorative elements to geometric panels.

Julia Morgan copied the grand entrance facade for William Randolph Hearst's Casa Grande at San Simeon from the fourteenth- to sixteenth-century Church of Santa Maria la Mayor, Ronda, Spain. Rendered in white Utah limestone, the facade is *Plateresco* in style but the overabundance of stone work, woodwork, iron balconies and tile give it a *Churrigueresco* appearance. The quatrefoil shape of the fountain is one of the many Gothic forms used throughout the house.

Opposite page
Top: The courtyard entrance of the Adamson House, 1928, Malibu, has a medieval story-and-a-half appearance adopted by many Spanish Revival houses. The projecting upper story is supported by beams and, along with the tower and bottle-glass windows, they create a medieval appearance.

Bottom left: The deep-set door of the Adamson House has bottle-glass panels and it is enhanced by a stone arch, decorative Malibu tiles and a Spanish Revival wall lamp with dragons' head and spike motifs.

Bottom right: Wallace Neff accentuated the entrance of the 1926 Drucker Residence, Los Angeles, by creating a pavilion, almost like a small chapel, with a gable, side finials and scrolls. The central arch entrance is defined with attached columns and a recessed metal-and-glass door.

The *Mudéjar*-patterned wooden entrance door to the Casa de Buena Vista, 1929-35, Montecito, is crowned by a tile panel.

Tiles, informally set into the plaster wall, flank the entrance door of the Casa de Buena Vista in Montecito. To the right is a grilled window, one of a pair that flanks the entrance.

A wooden *Mudéjar*-patterned door with a central star is found at the Andalusia Apartments, 1926, Hollywood, by owners-designers Arthur and Nina Zwebel.

Casa del Sol, one of the guest houses which Julia Morgan designed for the Hearst estate at San Simeon, 1919-47, is Moorish in design. Angular Moorish details distinguish the overdoor of the elaborate gilded entrance and the panels of the side door, left. "Craft Built" is the term Morgan used to refer to the work of the team of craftsmen who incorporated imported elements or mimicked the Old World styles. German ironworker Ed Trinkkeller, from Los Angeles, made the gilded wrought iron grills. The cornice tiles were produced by Deer Creek Potters.

The side door of the Hearst guest house, Casa del Sol, San Simeon, is decorated with interlace patterns over a gilded background. The metal Moorish-patterned door handle is also "Craft Built" by the local team of craftsmen.

Exotic Persian tiles surround the ornate entrance to Hearst's Casa del Sol, San Simeon. For millionaire Hearst, even the grout is gilded between the imported tiles.

Top left: Within the arch of Neff's Drucker House entrance, the glass-and-wrought iron door is a work of Los Angeles craftsman Julius Dietzmann. Guardian dogs decorate the lower door panels.

Top right: When viewed from the dining room, a deep arch frames the glass-and-wrought iron door of the Drucker House from the inside. The pattern of the door is particularly enjoyed when outside light emphasizes the decorative silhouettes. The Spanish Revival chandelier is decorated with dragons.

Wallace Neff created a subtle entrance pavilion at the Thomson Residence, Beverly Hills, by setting it off from the volume of the house with tapered attached columns. Under the bougainvillea, finials capped the columns creating a "gable chapel" motif entrance as at Neff's Drucker House.

The Thomson Residence had a monumental stone door surround, with a common Mexican *Churrigueresco* motif, a decorative border ending in a circular spiral.

Iron craftsman Julius Dietzmann used sunflowers as the theme for the pattern of the Thomson Residence's wrought iron-and-glass entrance doors. Dietzmann included his favorite "guard dog" motif.

From the Thomson Residence's double-height entrance hall, the door's pattern of sunflowers and guard dogs can be easily appreciated due to reflected light from the courtyard. Here, also are wrought iron air vents flanking the door and a Spanish style turned wood balcony rail.

Another wrought iron-and-glass door by Julius Dietzmann depicts elegant potted plants. It opens to the east garden of Neff's Drucker Residence.

The mid-1920s Cottrell Residence by Gordon Kaufmann, Los Angeles, features a wrought iron entrance door. Without any glazing, the entrance atrium has an outdoor feeling.

Broad glass-and-metal doors with grape vine motifs open out to the south terrace and the ocean view visible from the Adamson House in Malibu.

GARDEN PASSAGES

The upper half of Casa del Herrero's kitchen courtyard door is opened with turned spindles that provide a view of the herb garden.

For the drive-through passage from the courtyard to the landscaped gardens of the Thomson House, Wallace Neff produced one of his characteristic pointed arches — slightly rounded and outlined in stone. The metal plaque, right, depicts a Spanish knight fighting a dragon.

From Casa del Herrero's herb garden, the courtyard door is decorated with an imported Spanish Gothic stone surround.

A garden wall, overgrown with hedges, at the Casa del Herrero is opened by a spindled garden door capped with a segmental arch, giving it the appearance of a cottage gate.

Passing from the Adamson House entrance courtyard to the gardens, greenhouses and the beach, the garages are finished in a grand fashion with a broad carved lintel and central door medallions. The outdoor bench is rendered in the same distinguished manner.

A slender wooden side door at Montecito's Casa del Herrero is finished in a simple Moorish pattern rendered in nail heads.

An awning shades a pair of garden doors at the Drucker House. Awnings and outdoor curtains were often a part of 1920s and 30s Spanish Revival houses, giving them a theatrical character.

Pocket doors and pocket screen doors open the dining room of the Drucker House to the east garden. Wallace Neff included this practical amenity throughout the house and in many of his other projects.

An arched door with spindled shutters leads from the living room of the Casa del Herrero to a garden room.

A garden room is viewed from the master suite of the Casa del Herrero, Montecito. It is furnished with a wall fountain and aluminum furniture designed by the resident, George Steedman. The tile paving is finished with decorative pavers.

The tiled wall fountain of Casa del Herrero's east garden room is set in a niche opened by a window and crowned by a wrought iron dragon.

Medieval castles and regal lions accent the Tunisian tile pavers of Casa del Herrero's east garden room.

Terrace steps formed the transition from the dining room wing of the
Thomson House to a garden divided into quadrants — a common garden
treatment from Spain's townhouses and haciendas.

Courtyard arcades — common to California since the Missions — are one of the most appealing aspects of the Spanish Revival house. This one at the Drucker House, is articulated by a chimney projection and tiles laid in a Moorish pattern.

The courtyard arcade at the 1926 Degnan House in La Cañada-Fintridge has a robust Spanish form also used at the El Paseo in Santa Barbara, 1922-23. Wrought iron plant holders and a glass star chandelier enhance the space.

The rear terrace of the Casa del Herrero is a
vaulted indoor-outdoor living room with a
painted dado, tile details, wrought iron window
grill and wall sconce. Original resident George
Steedman designed the aluminum furniture.
The tile wall niche is a Moorish invention.

The exotic patterns of Spain's Moorish style decorate
the rear terrace of the Casa del Herrero. Antiques
dealers Arthur and Mildred Byne imported the
Moorish niche with intricate wood doors
for the Steedmans.

Casa del Herrero's rear terrace extends into the south garden and provides a place for dining on George Steedman's aluminum table and armchairs.

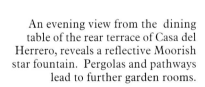

An evening view from the dining table of the rear terrace of Casa del Herrero, reveals a reflective Moorish star fountain. Pergolas and pathways lead to further garden rooms.

A close view of one of George Steedman's outdoor armchairs show that he rendered a Spanish style quilted leather-and-wood chair in aluminum. The central crest and figures incised in the front apron make Steedman family associations.

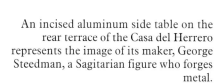

An incised aluminum side table on the rear terrace of the Casa del Herrero represents the image of its maker, George Steedman, a Sagitarian figure who forges metal.

The Adamson House on Malibu beach
includes many outdoor spaces, including a
kitchen courtyard, walled on one side. It is
decorated with a tile panel of heraldic
peacocks and flanking windows protected
by a grill of turned wooden spindles.

Another courtyard at the Adamson
House, Malibu, is a large working area
between the garages and the kitchen area.
It is a paved area defined by a rustic,
curved brick wall accented by stones and
enhanced by a tile wall fountain.

The flagstone-paved kitchen courtyard of the Casa del Herrero, Montecito, is made more inviting by the addition of a built-in tile bench.

The bench of the Casa del Herrero's kitchen courtyard is accompanied by a pointed arch window secured by a metal grill. The Moorish stepped border pattern tile is repeated throughout the dadoes of the house.

Within Casa del Herrero's herb garden, the pointed arch window opens the garden wall to the kitchen courtyard. Below it, a built-in tile garden seat overlooks the garden.

Pergolas are regular features of Spanish gardens and one at Casa del Herrero, Montecito, provides a tile seat and tile paving. The seat back features large side scrolls.

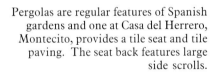

A decorative Tunisian paver under the pergola of the Casa del Herrero renders a medieval castle in two popular Spanish colors, turquoise and terracotta.

On Malibu beach, the Adamson House has two semi-circular garden rooms terraced into the landscape. They are rustic in character with flagstone paving and stone-and-concrete seats.

One of the garden rooms at the Adamson House features a concrete seat made to appear like stone. The barbecue pit was a gift to the Adamsons from Will Rogers.

Spanish Revival garden rooms are fit into the curves of a landscape, as at the Adamson House, or arranged along an axis in the Moorish tradition, as at the Casa del Herrero. The south garden of the Montecito estate has several waterworks and paved garden rooms along its axis.

Built-in tile seating, aluminum furnishings and a tile fountain create a gracious outdoor space near the south end of the Casa del Herrero garden.

The swimming pool and pool house at the Malibu Adamson House form another enjoyable outdoor space common to Spanish Revival homes of Southern California.

The hacienda-style pool house of the Adamson House owes its character to its one-story, tile-roof form and central porch.

Top left: Simple bracket columns uphold the beam ceiling of the pool house porch, which is paved with Malibu tiles. Stored there is a once lovely, tile-and-wrought iron table that has eroded after years of exposure to the ocean air.

Top right: The Adamson pool house porch is enhanced by a fireplace and grill, and a painted mural by Danish artists Ejnar Hansen and Peter Nielsen, depicting conquistadors, Gaspar de Portola and his men, claiming the California coast for Spain in 1769. The wrought iron grill is finished with copper details that have oxidized to appear green.

Left: The Adamson House fence separating the pool and pool house from the beach is an unusual design. Chevrons run along the top bar and star patterns repeat in each panel of the metal and wire fence. Turned-wood balusters separate each panel.

Used for a public purpose, this pleasurable pavilion on Catalina Island is an inspiring form for domestic Spanish Revival garden rooms and poolhouses. It is a rest stop along the route from Crescent Beach to the Catalina Casino.

The recently renovated Catalina pavilion was designed in a Mission form displaying colorful Catalina tiles, popular throughout the 1920s, '30s and '40s.

Decorating the Garden Room

Southern California Tiles

California inherited a legacy from Spanish, Moorish and Mexican ceramic centers, like Seville and Talavera de la Reina in Spain, and Puebla in Mexico. Those production centers perpetuated the *Mudéjar* patterns steeped into all of Spain's decorative arts, and they also expressed other foreign influences, particularly from Italian *majolica*, French *faience* and Dutch Delftware. Both the Spanish and the Moors had absorbed ceramic techniques and formal influences long before Californian and Mexican production, producing decorative tiles by many methods, including incising, stamping and rouletting with a tool for texture. However, the three most popular methods were *cuerda seca*, *cuenca* and painted tile.

The *cuerda seca*, or dry cord, technique (also called Moorish) produced a dark charred line separating the colors of a design at the juncture where the glazes would meld together. On the other hand, the *cuenca* method (also called Saracen) made a softer transition between colors. *Cuenca* means "tub" and the color glazes were inlaid into impressions made in the clay, creating ridges that separate the colors. The third type are simply tiles painted after glazing.

While many Californians imported their tiles from Spain, Tunisia, Portugal and Mexico, numerous kilns and tile companies opened in the 1920s to accommodate the many public and private structures built in the Spanish style. Although tile production was complex with companies frequently changing ownership and designers, three key characters stand out as shaping the general direction of Southern California's tilework. The first is Arts and Crafts master Ernest Batchelder, whose Craftsman tiles of muted browns, blues, and ochres decorated many fireplaces of Mission and Spanish style houses. Second was Fred Robertson, who began Claycraft Potteries and continued the fine techniques and matte finishes of Batchelder. Third is Rufus Keeler, who started "Calco," considered the predecessor of Malibu Potteries, which he managed. While Batchelder designed quaint Arts and Crafts cottage motifs, Robertson and Keeler actively pursued Hispano-Moresque designs.

By the mid-1920s, the greatest amount of mass-produced tiles in Southern California are generally attributed to three companies: Gladding McBean (It produced "Franciscan" dinnerware; and bought out Tropico Potteries and Catalina Clay Products, among others. The company began in 1875, in Lincoln, and still exists but no longer produces the 1920s-1930s tile and pottery.); American Encaustic Tiling Company (a Zanesville, Ohio and New York City company, which bought out West Coast Tile and California China Products, which had produced the Spanish style tiles for the 1915 San Diego exposition buildings); and California Clay Products, known as Calco (which was run by Rufus Keeler and had assumed his Southern California Clay Products).

In 1926, May Rindge asked Keeler to manage a new tile company she started, Malibu Potteries, and thus, Keeler's Calco became, in a sense, the predecessor for the new enterprise, although Calco and Malibu are distinctly different companies.

In fact, Malibu Potteries (also referred to as "Malibu Tile"), as well as the Catalina

A Spanish Revival mural decorates the rear courtyard of the Casa de Buena Vista in Montecito. It is in the style of Francisco Niculoso, an Italian who worked in Seville in the 1490s and whose Renaissance figurative style and decorative borders were copied by Spanish tile makers for centuries.

Clay Products Company (commonly called "Catalina Tile") have become the two best-known artistic names in Southern California tile production during the 1920s and 30s era. This is due to the identity of their owners, the quality of their works and the significant commissions or placement of their works.

Malibu Potteries was begun by May Rindge, who, with her husband, Frederick, owned Spanish land grant property and developed the Malibu area. Their pottery company produced tiles for many Los Angeles-area buildings, such as the City Hall and Mayan Theatre. The majority of their tiles followed the Spanish trend and they manufactured the Spanish-style tiles for the Malibu house of their daughter, Rhoda, and her husband, Merrit Adamson. However, despite Malibu Potteries' prolific output and esteemed reputation, the company operated briefly, from 1926 until 1932, closing shortly after a 1931 fire destroyed the factory.

Catalina Clay Products was associated with the development of Catalina Island by William Wrigley, Jr. In Chicago, Wrigley had established his gum company, Wrigley Field and a baseball team, and on Catalina, he developed the small Spanish-Deco city of Avalon, where he built a vacation home, a practice field and cottages for his team. To construct bricks, pavers and roof tiles for his development projects, Wrigley started a construction company and, by 1929, produced casual and colorful glazed tiles. Shortly after, individual clients requested Catalina tiles and pottery for other buildings on the mainland as well. While in its heydey, the company produced the influential Avalon city fountains, street works and bird plaques but, like Malibu Potteries, the Catalina company was short-lived; in 1937, it was bought out by Gladding McBean.

The south terrace of the Degnan House in La Cañada-Flintridge features a tile niche treated like a stain-glass window with a glazed terracotta roundel of the Virgin and Child in the della Robbia style. One of the family of Florentine sculptors, Girolamo della Robbia, traveled to Spain in the early sixteenth century and influenced that country's taste for these relief figures.

Architect Julia Morgan and her client William Randolph Hearst made many trips to Europe for items like the Persian tile mural decorating the Casa del Sol guest house. Persian-style tiles by local Deer Creek Potters decorate the door surrounds. Also, note the tiles and cast stone ornament capping the chimney. John van der Loo and his father, Theo, produced the cast stone work at the San Simeon workshop.

Tunisian tiles were specially made for the Casa del Herrero, Montecito, under the direction of Arthur Byne and Mildred Stapley Byne, former curators at New York's Hispanic Society of America. A garden room focuses on an elaborate tile niche depicting a floral urn framed by a horseshoe arch.

Imported Tunisian tiles also finish the built-in benches flanking the ornate niche of one of Casa del Herrero's garden room.

A terrace of the Adamson House, Malibu, features a decorative panel designed in similar motifs as the Tunisian tile mural in the garden niche of the Casa del Herrero in Montecito. Unlike Spanish and Tunisian imports with light backgrounds and a preference for blue and yellow, the designs of Malibu Potteries tended to use all-over patterns and a preference for turquoise and terracotta hues.   Here, also, are paneled shutters, a wrought iron window box and Gothic chimney of a style for an outdoor fireplace.

A multi-tile parrot mural was featured on a garden wall of the Thomson Residence, Beverly Hills, which was decorated with tiles from Gladding McBean.

A single macaw with a turquoise border decorates a wall of the El Encanto Market on Catalina. Catalina Clay Products tended to use many single color tiles in their designs and, in their simplicity, they expressed a great vitality that worked well with Catalina's Moderne and Art Deco architectural interpretations of the Spanish Revival style.

Two parrots are represented in a mural from Catalina's El Encanto Market. Roger "Bud" Upton created the bird motifs and a bird sanctuary on Catalina likely led to the popularity of the bird murals made by Catalina Clay Products. The murals were also framed and sold as popular tourist items, and sold in Los Angeles on Olvera Street (the oldest street in the Mexican heart of the city) and at the Biltmore Hotel in Phoenix, Arizona — a hotel which Catalina's developer William Wrigley, Jr. owned.

Fish decorate a four-panel underwater vista found on a fountain at the El Encanto Market. Images of aquatic life were appropriate to the island-based Catalina Clay Products which produced the mural.

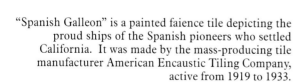

"Spanish Galleon" is a painted faience tile depicting the proud ships of the Spanish pioneers who settled California. It was made by the mass-producing tile manufacturer American Encaustic Tiling Company, active from 1919 to 1933.

The large tile and ceramic manufacturing firm, Gladding McBean, produced a pair of metal-framed, *cuerda seca* murals, circa 1930. This one is known as "Senor" or "The Guitar Player."

Matching "Senor" is "Senorita," or "The Dancer," also by Gladding McBean, circa 1930. Note the dress style of the figures in both murals and the crested frames with central crosses, imparting a formal Spanish feeling to the revival works.

Pomona Tile Manufacturing Company (1923-66) produced this "Sailing Ship" *cuenca* tile, featuring a painterly version of the Spanish galleon at sea.

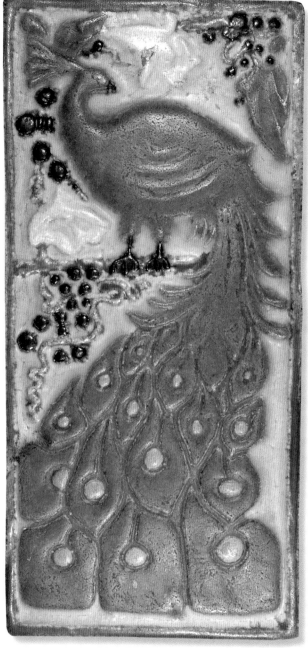

A peacock hearth tile is a painted relief work with a matte glaze, produced by Rufus Keeler's company, Calco, or California Clay Products. Keeler began the company in 1923 and it continued the work of his Southern California Clay Products, which he had begun in 1917. Eventually Keeler left Calco to manage Malibu Potteries in 1926.

Parrots and heraldic dragons decorate this rectangular Gothic style painted relief tile produced by Malibu Potteries, 1926-32.

One of Southern California's leading tile makers, Fred Robertson, manufactured this Moorish style geometric interlace tile by the *cuenca* method at his Claycraft Potteries, 1921-36.

An arabesque interlace pattern was one of many Moorish-inspired works produced by Malibu Potteries, 1926-32, under the management and artistic direction of Rufus Keeler.

FOUNTAINS

Along the terraced axis of Casa del Herrero's south garden, a Moorish-style fountain is more than decoration; it is a defining landscape feature. The ground-level rivulet passes from basin to basin through the garden.

A detail shows the water flow of Casa del Herrero's rivulet as it passes from one level to another. Tiles for the fountain were imported from Tunisia.

The main feature of the terrace of the Cottrell Residence in Los Angeles is a wall fountain with a vase for its basin. Portuguese tiles surround the dolphins in relief.

Gladding McBean tiles decorate a wall fountain at the Thomson Residence. The basin is clad in sunflower tiles, a motif that was repeated in other tiles and wrought iron detail throughout the house designed by Wallace Neff.

The Peacock Fountain at the Adamson House is a wall type fountain produced by Malibu Potteries. Its design follows the curved shape of the low courtyard wall and creates a central background panel for the vase-fountain with the curves of the flanking peacocks following the outline curves of the upper wall.

A vase on a pedestal provides the focus for the Adamson House heraldic peacocks as well as its water source.

The Adamson House Neptune Fountain is located on a concave curved courtyard wall defining a side courtyard. Tiles, relief sculpture and basin are produced by Malibu Potteries.

Among Spanish-style freestanding fountains, the Gothic quatrefoil form is a favorite. At the Andalusia Apartments, that form is elaborated with a central star and garden parterres.

In keeping with the Moorish star pattern fountain, an outdoor fireplace at the Andalusia Apartments is in the form of a Moorish pointed arch. These pleasurable amenities were designed by Arthur and Nina Zwebell, original owners and designers of the court-yard apartments.

The Spanish-Moorish tiles of Andalusia's fountain present lively interpretations of the traditional patterns, while using the pure Spanish colors — predominantly blue, white and yellow.

A quatrefoil-shaped fountain located at the large garden room of Casa del Herrero's south garden features colorful Tunisian tiles and an unusual pedestal spout.

The Arabic star form is used for a fountain on the grounds of the Adamson House. Well-defined patterns of the Malibu Potteries tile seem appropriate for the fountain's geometric shape.

On Catalina island, Avalon's plaza fountain presents an octagonal basin and monumental pedestal displaying the casual Moderne character of the Catalina tiles.

The pedestal of the Avalon fountain shows Catalina Tile's Moorish interlace tiles and solid color tiles.

Among practical tile works, the Adamson House features a courtyard dog bath decorated with floral and geometric patterned Malibu tiles.

An outdoor mud sink in the kitchen courtyard of the Casa del Herrero is decorated with a delightful display of figurative and decorative Tunisian tile.

WALLS

Tiles and tile panels decorate many Spanish Revival garden walls and outer parameter walls. The outer walls of the Adamson House face the Pacific Coast Highway in Malibu and are marked with tiles from Malibu Potteries.

Among the tiles on the Adamson House wall is an incised Mayan-style tile that Malibu Potteries produced for the Mayan Theatre.

Catalina tiles are set informally into the plaster border of an Avalon Bay wall overlooking the island city's marina.

The Adamson House courtyard wall is highlighted with a baroque curve and is outlined in red tile.

A scalloped terrace wall, like many found in Spain and Mexico, provided an authentic Spanish vernacular element at the 1923-25 Thomson House in Beverly Hills.

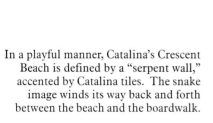

In a playful manner, Catalina's Crescent Beach is defined by a "serpent wall," accented by Catalina tiles. The snake image winds its way back and forth between the beach and the boardwalk.

The head of Catalina's serpent wall is rendered with a toothy grimace, a scowling eye and a ridged forehead — all rendered in brick and tile.

Catalina's serpent wall, lined with benches, ends in a tight coil. While the coil shape is reminiscent of a snake's rattle, the stepped or spiraled motif is also an ancient Moorish one.

A wall defining a Spanish Revival courtyard may not be freestanding but a structural wing, treated in an innovative manner. A wing of the Casa de Buena Vista appears like a village wall following a road to the central plaza, when it is actually the driveway passing a wing of the house and arriving at the entrance motor court.

An arched opening in the courtyard wall of the Andalusia Apartments presents tile stair risers and an arched entrance to the rear terrace, furnished with a stone table and fountain.

At the Thomson House, architect Wallace Neff enlivened the central courtyard with an outdoor staircase. A stepped wall followed the stairs making a dramatic silhouette against the white stucco wall. The enclosing trellis was added later.

A Spanish Revival courtyard wall was frequently enhanced with a fireplace, like the one with a pointed arch and flanking sconces at the Andalusia Apartments.

PAVING

Spanish Revival paving on terraces, *corredors* and *portales* is usually tile, frequently with decorative pavers, as seen on the east terrace of the Adamson House. There, the threshold is defined with broken tiles and pottery, following a traditional device used by the Spanish to keep away evil spirits.

The Adamson House east terrace includes decorative tiles for a step riser to the interior, left, and a planter, right.

The hexagonal blue griffin tile from Malibu Potteries is the primary decorative paver for the Adamson House's east terrace.

Flagstone paving is common for many medium to large size Spanish Revival courtyards — for dining terraces to motor courts, as at the Thomson Residence, Beverly Hills.

At the Adamson House, the entrance courtyard is paved in flagstone with grass borders, a pleasant combination of landscaping and paving.

Flagstone courtyards can be organized into patterns as this one in a motor court of the Degnan House. It is an encircled star with grass borders.

The paving of the entrance courtyard at the Casa del Herrero is made of pebbles and it is copied from the Moorish Patio de la Reja at the Alhambra Palace in Granada, Spain.

A detail of the entrance courtyard paving of Casa del Herrero displays a fortress and interlace and chevron border patterns.

Heraldic birds are also depicted in pebbles in the entrance courtyard of Montecito's Casa del Herrero.

Pebble paving is also used around one of the public fountains at Avalon decorated with Catalina Tile. The paving, in a circular pattern, also includes stone, brick and tile detail.

In Spain and Arab countries, the Islamic *mushrabiyah* allowed one to have filtered air and light and a view of the outdoors while being screened from view. The window form also followed Western European Gothic concepts to garner needed space from areas above streets and corridors. The gilded *mushrabiyah* at the Casa del Sol guesthouse of the Hearst Estate, San Simeon, displays fine *Mudéjar*-styled *artesonado*. The carved woodwork includes interlace pattern screens, corbels in baroque patterns and inset tiles.

Mudéjar-style woodwork graces a balcony on the entrance facade of Casa de las Campanas, Los Angeles. It features balcony panels carved in geometric patterns and bold bracket columns – common to historic structures in Spain and Arab countries. The wall lamp is in the shape of an Arabic hanging incense burner.

A cast stone balcony at the Casa Grande, San Simeon, is accented by a heraldic lion, medieval-style figurative panels, and "putti" corbels that seem to uphold the whole balcony. Made of concrete and white sand, the castings appear like stone. "Craft Built," the stonework was cast by Theo and John van der Loo, part of the Hearst Castle team.

Standing sentinel over Casa Grande is a cast two-foot-high stone lion that highlights Hearst Castle's rear balcony overlooking the San Simeon countryside.

The *Plateresco* entrance door of the Degnan House is marked by a balcony decorated by a scalloped shell on the underside.

A Spanish style corner bedroom balcony at the Andalusia Apartments features Spanish Revival woodwork: a roof cornice with moldings and dentils, and turned columns and balusters.

The rear courtyard of the Casa de Buena Vista, Montecito, features a long balcony that is flanked by side wings. This type, which runs continuously along any wing of a Spanish Revival house, tends to be called, incorrectly, a "Monterey" type. However, it is stained wood, not painted, and does not continue across the facade or continue around the sides of the house, like the original Monterey balconies did.

Casa del Herrero includes a vernacular Spanish bedroom balcony with turned balusters and a bracket column. The ends of the beams are festively decorated as kitten faces.

Above the Thomson House entrance is an iron-and-tile balcony, a type common to many entrances of Spanish Revival houses.

A view from the entrance porch of the Thomson House provides a fine display of Spanish Revival tiles. The sunflower style tiles were made by Gladding McBean.

One balcony at the Casa del Herrero is made of iron with a platform made of tile in a simple blue-and-white check pattern. Above, two scalloped courses form the roof cornice and repeat the arched shape of the roof tile.

Teakwood and stone cornices on Hearst's Casa Grande are decorated in a fanciful way with a combination of *Churrigueresco* ornament, mythic characters and heraldic emblems. The teakwood was so rare that it took five years to complete the work by "Craft Built" woodworker Jules Suppo, assisted by Fred Jordan.

A comparison of eaves and cornices on the unfinished backside of the Hearst estate shows the simple concrete treatment of one wing next to the ornate sculptural character of Casa Grande's teakwood cornice.

The Casa del Sol guesthouse at the Hearst estate offers decorative elements hidden under the eaves. Cast stone putti and sculptural ornament is Craft Built by Theo and John van der Loo.

PIERCED WALLS AND CHIMNEY STACKS

Under the teakwood eaves of the rear facade of Casa Grande, a cast stone Gothic facade features two- and three-light windows. Pierced quatrefoil spandrels fill the space in between the pointed arch openings of the rear terrace.

On the entrance facade of the Degnan House, pierced elements — window and balcony — are of the same material and continuous with the wall.

Pierced grills would frequently cover bathroom windows as this one at the Drucker House in Los Angeles. An overall pattern of ceramic arches is decorated with a central *fleur de lis*.

Peacocks in a heraldic form, flanking a central column, decorate an imported Spanish pierced window at the Casa del Herrero.

In the indoor-outdoor hallways of Hearst's Casa Grande, pierced grills provide light yet offer privacy to the guest bedroom suites.

Chimney stacks of Spanish Revival houses can offer decorative piercing or interesting brickwork. At the Adamson House in Malibu, angular brickwork is repeated and stepped up for crowning the chimney. Also note the regal outdoor lamp rendered in wrought iron and purple glass.

Casa del Herrero features a pierced chimney stack in the gabled form of a tile-roof house. On the wall below, stone Gothic-style windows almost appear that they are pierced, since their sculptural form cuts into the thick wall.

Windows and Window Grills

Casa del Herrero's Gothic window with a dragon ornamented grill is located on the octagonal library. The room was added to the house in 1931 by Lutah Maria Riggs, George Washington Smith's talented associate, who took over unfinished projects in Smith's office when he died in 1930.

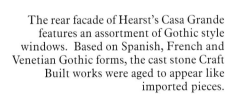

The rear facade of Hearst's Casa Grande features an assortment of Gothic style windows. Based on Spanish, French and Venetian Gothic forms, the cast stone Craft Built works were aged to appear like imported pieces.

A detail of one of Casa Grande's Gothic double-light window — decorated with medieval imagery — shows the creamy white stone of the window surround set against the gray concrete wall.

Cast red clay from Malibu Potteries was used for the stone-like surround for the elaborate four-part living room window on the south facade of the Adamson House.

A detail of the upper portion of the Adamson House living room window shows the smooth character of the cast ceramic. Also shown is a partially inset wall lamp, made with *Plateresco-Churrigueresco* style metal ornament and opaque glass.

Moorish style stained wood detailing and Moorish-patterned leaded glass mullions decorate the Anglo form of a bay window on the facade of the Casa de las Campanas.

Pointed arch windows decorate the side wings of the Adamson House's east facade. The broad form of this Moorish type arch is allegedly derived from Arabic city passages widened to accommodate donkeys and their side packs.

An inset circular window in a gable of the Adamson House is surrounded with Malibu tiles and in-filled with an ornate ceramic grate.

Paired arched windows with lower tile panels were a common window form on Spanish Revival houses. They were likely copied from the many Spanish architecture and decorative arts books published in America in the 1920s. Below is a deeply inset window protected by wire grill, affixed to the wall like a cage. Another notable element of Spanish houses is the window shutter. Here, pairs of wooden shutters flank all three windows and they are ornamented with small crosses.

Window grills copied from Spain frequently were crested and crowned with the Catholic symbol of the cross, as this one from the front facade of the Casa del Herrero.

A crested and cross crowned grill from the
Casa del Herrero fits into a window
overgrown with vines on the front wall of
the house. It opens into the niche of the
east garden room.

At the Drucker House in Los
Angeles, architect Wallace Neff
worked with metal craftsman
Julius Dietzmann to replicate
Spanish style window grills in
Southern California Spanish
Revival fashion. A pair of
grills on the west terrace show
the crested form along with an
ornate scroll border.

Spanish Revival crested and cross-crowned grills also appear at George Washington Smith's Casa de Buena Vista, like this one on the facade facing the entrance courtyard.

Along the entrance drive to the Casa de Buena Vista, Spanish Revival grills are convex in shape, as they bow out from the wall. Scrolls at the top and bottom are the only ornament.

Viewed straight on, Casa de Buena Vista's entrance drive grills curve upward at the top and curve downward below with the scroll decoration visible at each corner.

Under the shadow of lush foliage at the courtyard of the Andalusia Apartments, another curved window grill is found. The bold Mexican *Churrigueresco* form bows out from the window at the base where scrolls secure the sides.

A simple bowed window grill form was located at the kitchen window of the Thomson House.

Plain wire window grills affixed to the wall on all sides were quite common to the Spanish Revival. The dark metal grids set against the white stucco walls is visually appealing, especially when the window grill might be accompanied by blossoming vines, as this one at the Casa del Herrero.

Some window grills could be treated as an integrated part of the wall structure by stucco, masonry or wood bases or crowns, like one window grill on the facade of Casa de Buena Vista.

Small scale grill windows that usually light an interior bath or closet provide opportunity for delightful accents on a Spanish Revival facade. The small grill window located near the entrance door of the Casa del Herrero is an imported one with three decorated iron bars and opaque glass.

Casa de Buena Vista features a grill capped with two arches and wire floral ornament above a tiny square window. The window is one of a pair that flank the front entrance door.

A palatial formal style is represented by the ornate gilded grills decorating the Casa del Sol guest house at San Simeon. Designed by Ed Trinkkeller, the grill's upper cresting features mythic birds flanking a heraldic shield. Scroll ornament forms decorative sheaves of gilded iron and the border is accented with *fleur de lis* patterns.

Window grills are occasionally found on Spanish Revival interiors as this one for an interior window in the entrance foyer of the Adamson House. Pointed elements flank the upper cresting and a tight scroll pattern marks the upper border. A pointed leaf appears as a motif throughout the grill.

Spanish Revival houses were also furnished with iron entrance gates, imported from Spain or Mexico or designed anew in a Spanish manner. At the Rew-Sharp house on the Coronado peninsula, the iron entrance gate reflects a tight spiral and lily motif from Moderne times and added later to the 1919 *Churrigueresco* house.

Metalwork - Practical and Decorative

A flying dragon creates a dramatic silhouette against the Santa Ynez mountains. It is one of a pair decorating an awning armature of a bedroom terrace at the Casa del Herrero.

The Adamson House east terrace is accented by a bell supported by a decorative metal bracket with a horse in silhouette.

Bell ringers are popular Spanish Revival items that were frequently imported from Spain to add decorative detail to the front entrance door. The one located at the Degnan House appears like an elegant bird with peaked head feathers and curved tail feathers that turn into the scroll bracket.

An imported bronze bell marks the entrance to the Drucker House. A dragon and interlaced dragon heads complete the intricate ornamentation.

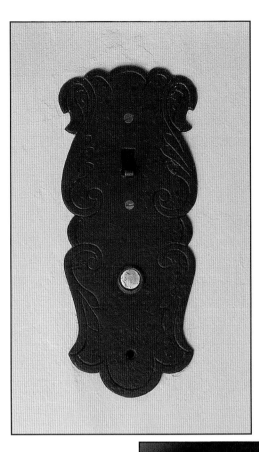

The bronze doorbell plate of the Drucker House is incised and creates a decorative outline against the light colored wall.

Regal bronze lions crafted by George Steedman for his house, Casa del Herrero, guard the house along the rear terrace rails.

Creating a bracket, the head of a royal peacock supports a wall lamp on a terrace of the Drucker House.

The lantern shape is a common one for Spanish Revival chandeliers and wall lamps on terraces and courtyards. The Casa del Sol at the Hearst estate has a hexagonal-sided wall lantern suspended from an ornate gilded bracket.

The Casa del Sol at the Hearst estate features a small rounded wall lantern hung at a corner location. Ironworker Ed Trinkkeller was frequently asked to reproduce imported pieces in Hearst's collection and he simulated an antique patina using decomposed limestone and oil.

Simple elegance dictates the bracket-supported Spanish Revival wall lanterns in the courtyard of the Andalusia Apartments.

Mudéjar metalwork style influenced the hanging wall lantern on the rear courtyard of the Casa de Buena Vista, Montecito.

A bracketed wall lantern is located at the entrance to the Degnan Residence. While *Mudéjar* geometric faceting likely influenced the glass shapes of the lantern, its crown ornament and scroll bracket reveals *Plateresco* motifs.

NICHES AND ALCOVES

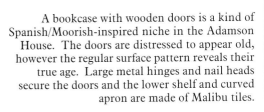

The niche and the window alcove were common Moorish forms of which inspiring examples could be copied from the Alhambra in Granada or in *Mudéjar* woodwork found throughout Spain. A niche in that tradition with carved wooden doors is in the Don and Alice Wilfong residence at the Andalusia Apartments. It is located in a secretive alcove under the arch of the staircase.

A bookcase with wooden doors is a kind of Spanish/Moorish-inspired niche in the Adamson House. The doors are distressed to appear old, however the regular surface pattern reveals their true age. Large metal hinges and nail heads secure the doors and the lower shelf and curved apron are made of Malibu tiles.

The Casa del Herrero features a bedroom window that is a tiled niche with built-in banquette seats on three sides. It is furnished with Moorish-patterned window shutters and an imported Spanish stool used as a table.

A common Western European style window seat can be also decorated in a Spanish-Moorish manner, like the one in the dining room of the Casa del Herrero. It's a shadowy, private place looking out to the rear terrace room and it is lined with Spanish tiles and can be closed by imported wooden shutters.

The Spanish Revival enjoyed the use of alcoves to dramatize the interior architecture or the specific use of a room. In a bedroom of the Casa de las Campanas, one arched alcove with a central oculus was planned for twin beds and a side table designed by Stickley Brothers. Also note the painted and carved beam ceiling, as well as the small pierced vents and the sconces, color coordinated with the furnishings.

A tiled banquette fits into a corner of a bedroom in the Casa de las Campanas. Above it is a window with Moorish patterned wood shutters and before it is a Spanish Revival stool that was produced by Stickley Brothers.

Casa del Herrero's breakfast room is furnished with an alcove for a tiled built-in credenza. Another alcove-like feature of the entire room is the change in floor height: the breakfast room is one step up from the adjacent kitchen. (A Spanish Revival spindle-fronted cabinet is located just inside the kitchen, right.) The walnut side chairs are fine Spanish examples of the seventeenth-to-eighteenth type that uses the arched architectural framework for its back and its front stretcher panel.

The guest bath of Casa del Herrero makes use of the alcove for the basin vanity. The alcove is accentuated by the arches of decorative tile and the under-sink opening. Furnishings that enhance the Spanish-Moorish style room are a gilded *Churrigueresco* mirror, Moorish-style hanging lanterns, and details like the drawer pulls, light switch, bell pull and pierced vent.

An arched alcove becomes the entire room at the Andalusia Apartments where the Zwebells used it to shape a bathroom. The shape of the room is emphasized by the wall painting. Sconces and chandelier are rendered in Moorish-faceted shapes.

STAIRCASES AND FIREPLACES

At the Casa del Herrero, an arch sets off the curved tiled staircase. A wrought iron rail follows the stair curve and is accented by a lion finial. Spanish furnishings here include a standing lamp adapted from a seventeenth century religious processional piece, and a chest with simple panels and a prominent base.

The staircase of the Zwebells' own original apartment at the Andalusia Apartments leads to a mezzanine library and the former office of Arthur Zwebell — now a bedroom. The stair defines one side of the double-height living room with an iron rail and tile risers. The fine Spanish, Arabic and European furnishings of Don and Alice Wilfong, who now own the apartments and reside here, are appropriate to the multi-cultural Spanish-Moorish architectural style.

A tiled Spanish kitchen fireplace was replicated for the master bedroom of Casa del Herrero. It includes a built-in tile seat and small fireplace located under the chimney canopy. Since early Spanish houses were warmed by Arabic braziers, Spanish kitchens first developed wall fireplaces like this one.

The library of Casa Grande included an imported stone fireplace. Although not Spanish, the Gothic style and monumental scale of the hearth of such western European fireplaces were copied in many Spanish Revival houses, especially when accompanied with Spanish style standing *luminarias*, as here.

A simulated stone fireplace is the focus of the guest bedroom of the Adamson House. Creating a small mantle is a Moorish-style niche decorated with Malibu tiles. Gilded triangular tiles surround the fireplace and the base is a mosaic of broken tile.

The fireplace in the living room of the Casa del Herrero is decorated by a grand Spanish crest. The fireplace is integral to the wall with the same stucco surfacing and the very slight projection of the chimney from the wall. The bronze Savanarola, or Dante, style chair with red velvet cushion is fourteenth century. Both the Spanish lyre-based Baroque table and the *vargueno* on its original trestle stand are seventeenth century.

The living room of the Adamson House features a Spanish Revival fireplace with a Moorish pointed arch. The canopy is decorated by Danish artists Ejnar Hansen and Peter Nielsen with a Neptune figure, respecting the house's beach location. The Spanish style andirons are in a bold baroque form.

The Spanish Revival Drucker House living room has a European style fireplace with a wide hearth and fireplace opening. However, the decorative detail of the stone over-mantle appears to follow Spanish *Plateresco*/Renaissance form with classical egg-and-dart and beaded detail, decorative brackets and columns as would be inspired by Spanish silverwork. The fireplace is seen through a multi-layered archway, one device that architect Wallace Neff frequently used to define a simple archway with light and shadow.

With a gilded molded cornice, slender classical columns, and scalloped metal shield, Spanish *Plateresco*/Renaissance sources likely inspired the fireplace of the Wilfong residence at the Andalusia Apartments. Flanking it are Moorish-style metal-and-glass sconces.

WALL, CEILING AND DOOR DECORATIONS

The library of the Casa Grande at the Hearst estate incorporates a Spanish ceiling with painted arches depicting historic and religious scenes. The spaces in between are filled with carved wood Moorish-patterned ceiling panels. Medieval elements and painting could fit comfortably into any Spanish Revival structures and be historically "accurate" since in Spain, medieval decorative arts and *Mudéjar* crafts lingered long throughout the country.

The bundled shafts of the Casa Grande Library beams start from the floor and separate the library bays. Figures and symbols fill the frames of the central shaft, while chevrons, dots and vine tendrils shape the borders. The bookshelves are Italian.

The guest bedroom of the Adamson House features Spanish Revival closet panels decorated with central floral motifs and door panels painted with overall baroque patterns. The decorative work was carried out by Danish émigré artists Ejnar Hansen and Peter Nielsen.

The staircase of the Casa del Herrero shows a painted dado bordered by tiles in a stepped Moorish motif. The baseboard is decorated with a band of solid tiles and a decorative border.

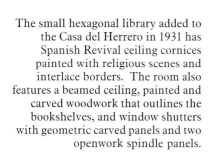

A wall beam in the children's bedroom of the Casa del Herrero was painted by George Steedman with a mural depicting the life of Saint Barbara, patron saint of the nearby city.

The small hexagonal library added to the Casa del Herrero in 1931 has Spanish Revival ceiling cornices painted with religious scenes and interlace borders. The room also features a beamed ceiling, painted and carved woodwork that outlines the bookshelves, and window shutters with geometric carved panels and two openwork spindle panels.

Spanish monastic choir stalls are used as panels for the dining room of the Casa Grande. Also called the refectory, the double-height room is furnished with monastic tables and Dante-style chairs. "Craft Built," the chairs were assembled by the local craft team from antique Spanish elements French & Company provided. The upholstery fabric is antique.

The entrance hall of the Casa del Herrero is finished with a ceiling imported from a fifteenth-century monastic house from the Convent of San Francisco, near Naranco, in the province of Tereul, Spain. In between the beams, are rectangular panels depicting various saints. The decorative detail surrounding each saint is rendered in black-and-red *Mudéjar* interlace.

At the Cottrell Residence in Los Angeles, Spanish Revival beams and panels are decorated in delicate *Plateresco* classical forms.

The library of the Drucker House has a beamed ceiling with the ceiling spans outlined and bordered in scroll patterns.

The ceiling of the Drucker House dining room features ornate panels defined by painted beams. Baroque borders and central motifs imitate carved and sculpted three-dimensional forms.

Square panels with stepped, three-dimensional gilded borders focus on Moorish motifs in the dining room ceiling of the Adamson House, Malibu.

Delicate floral patterns and small putti decorate the repeated vaults of an Adamson House hallway.

An imported Moorish ceiling crowns the rear entrance hall of the Casa Grande, San Simeon. The central section is made up of geometric interlace patterns surrounding a faceted roundel.

Doors were easily imported from Spain for Spanish Revival houses like the grand *Mudéjar* wood doors leading to the master suite of the Casa del Herrero. The geometric patterns are crowned with robust *Churrigueresco* cresting and flourishes. The flanking sconces are upheld by simple scrolls and *cuenca* tiles form a wall dado for the upstairs hallway.

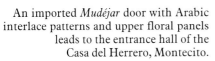

An imported *Mudéjar* door with Arabic interlace patterns and upper floral panels leads to the entrance hall of the Casa del Herrero, Montecito.

Casa Grande's guestrooms were entered through indoor-outdoor hallways. The shadowy halls are lit with hanging lanterns. Wooden doors are accented with Spanish style iron hinges and hardware treated to appear aged.

The Hearst craftsmen created Spanish style wood doors, like these, with exaggerated metal hardware, along all the hallways of the Casa Grande.

One guestroom in the south deck of the Casa Grande features a "Craft Built" three-paneled wood door screen.

The three-paneled door screen of the Casa Grande guestroom opens to a Talavera tiled bath.

Leather was frequently used in Spain for screens and doors with Cordova as the main production center. The kitchen door at the Wilfong residence in the Andalusia Apartments is a worn leather-covered door with Moorish patterns defined in brass nail heads.

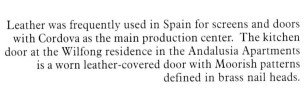

Metalwork: Lighting, Decorative and Practical Hardware

An imported Spanish silver chandelier, with candlestick-lights, decorates the morning room of Hearst's Casa Grande. The ceiling is Spanish.

The rear entrance hall of the Casa Grande features an imported Spanish silver chandelier in a formal Moorish influenced style.

A circular hallway of the Cottrell Residence features a tin star chandelier. The star form is a popular Arabic shape that has been reproduced for many Spanish and Mexican lamps.

A Moorish-style hanging lantern made of glass and metal is located in the dining room on the ground floor of the circular tower of the Andalusia Apartments.

The circular beamed ceiling of the upper tower room of the Andalusia Apartments — Arthur Zwebell's former office — features a faceted Spanish Revival lantern.

A medieval style lamp with iron ring, chains and candles hangs in a stair tower of the Casa Grande at the Hearst estate.

The narrow stairway leading to the guest bedrooms of the Casa Grande features a lantern-style wall sconce hanging from a wood-and-metal bracket. The lantern is distinguished by delicate metalic leaves.

In the children's bedroom of the Casa del Herrero, a lantern-style sconce is upheld by a bracket decorated with a wire tree-of-life inhabited by two birds.

A *Churrigueresco*-style sconce in the dining room of the Casa del Herrero features a gilded decorative plaque magnifying the light of an electrified candle held by a gilded vase. The crested side chair is Spanish seventeenth century.

The peacock motif used throughout the Drucker House forms the focus of an iron wall sconce lit by two electrified candles.

Metal is used to create the foliate silhouettes on the light shade as well as form the bracket of one wall sconce at the Cottrell Residence, Los Angeles.

Medieval style is applied to the wall plaque and candle bases of a sconce in the living room of the Cottrell Residence. The pair of electrified candles are covered by shades.

Shaded sconces are featured in the living room of the Adamson House. Foliate shapes decorate the arms and wall plate of the triple candle lamp. In the hallway, left, is a chandelier with a glass shade suspended by chains and ornamented with projecting metal filigree. The hallway also includes an interior grilled window and carpets of tile.

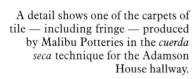

A detail shows one of the carpets of tile — including fringe — produced by Malibu Potteries in the *cuerda seca* technique for the Adamson House hallway.

Drapery rods and drapery brackets were commonly elaborated in black wrought iron in Spanish and Spanish Revival houses. This drapery rod in the dining room of the Casa del Herrero is punctuated with wiry vegetative forms.

The drapery rods in the dining room tower of the Andalusia Apartments was subtly curved to accommodate the round room. The rods spiral at the end and they are finished in a flower. At the wall, the drapery brackets are also finished in a flower form. Draperies in Spanish style houses tend to be made in rich fabrics like velvet, silk or satin.

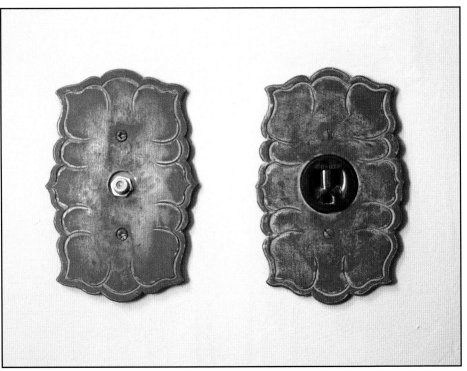

Even the electric and cable plates at the Drucker House are incised and form decorative silhouettes.

The iron drapery brackets at the Drucker House are designed in foliate forms that appear animated.

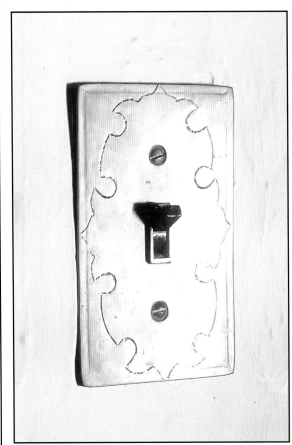

Air vents at the Andalusia Apartments are cast iron with interlaced patterns and decorated borders.

The switch plates (and electric plates) at the Andalusia Apartments are polished brass with incised decorative patterns.

At the Drucker House, the built-in library cabinets are finished in hardware designed for the house by Julius Dietzmann who completed all of its decorative metalwork.

A close view of the bronze lion finial that George Steedman designed for his home reveals its raised paw, incised main and decorated base. Its form is the same one Steedman used for the rear terrace rail finials.

Spanish Revival Rooms and Furniture Details

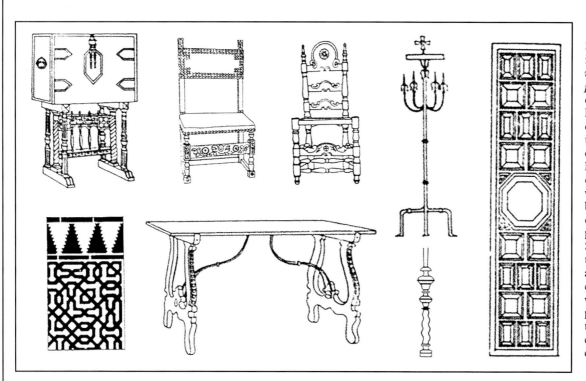

Spanish furniture forms include chests called *varguenos*, similar to *papallerias* (writing tables) except that they have a drop-leaf writing area. Other common forms are: trestle table with lyre supports, crested wood chair, luminarias, and chests with decorative panels. Spindles, wood panels, nail heads and brass tacks were used decoratively, as well as practically, for construction. Spanish furniture continued the Moorish *Mudéjar* style, and walnut was the most commonly used wood. Books with Spanish furniture were printed more frequently in the 1920s in America coinciding with the revival of their forms.

One of the story-and-a-half guest rooms of the Casa Grande features a Spanish style stair and "Craft Built" Spanish Revival doors. Architect and designer Julia Morgan characteristically mixed different styles of imported furnishings into a harmonious eclectic design. While Italy, England and France are represented in many of the furniture pieces, the spiral column and spiral balusters are also *Churrigueresco* style and the brazier is an Arabic feature included in Spanish Revival interiors.

Opposite page, bottom
Hexagonal red tile flooring and a beamed ceiling define the large living room of the Casa del Herrero. Most of its furnishings are Spanish imports, such as the *Mudéjar* style double door, right, and the window shutters, far wall. Groupings of furniture are loosely arranged around two Spanish walnut lyre-based tables at each end of the room. In the foreground, a bronze Dante-style chair is decorated with finials, decorative side panels and red velvet back and cushion. Left, a leather back Friarlero style chair is decorated with brass nail heads and star patterns. On buying trips to Spain, Arthur and Mildred Byne helped the Steedmans and architect George Washington Smith to furnish the room, and the entire house. A Spanish Revival record player was fitted into a Moorish-style niche, left foreground.

The dining room of the Casa del Herrero features a Spanish Revival setting, including the tile floor, beam ceiling, tiled stair and medieval style corner fireplace decorated by George Steedman with a Sagitarian image. Spanish imported furnishings include the door, right, dining table, nineteenth century Catalonian crested chairs and eighteenth century chest.

Interior designer John Holtzclaw purchased Spanish Revival style furniture for the Adamson House from Barker Brothers. In the dining room are leather upholstered chairs surrounding the table. The medieval style chandelier is a ring with multiple candles. The room is accented with a fireplace in a Moorish pointed arch form with a simple projecting over-mantle. Note also the iron drapery rods that end in dynamic spirals.

The dining room of the Adamson House is completed with a Barker Brothers Spanish Revival credenza. It is decorated with gilded chevron patterns and central door panels with gilded foliate motifs. Its wood is treated to appear aged and the hardware is decoratively over-scaled. The gilded mirror frame is ornamented with festive baroque forms. Metal tacks holding the chairs' leather backs are made into decorative elements and the front stretcher panels show geometric piercing. The red tile floor, decorative border and baseboard is made of Malibu tile.

The 1920s kitchen of the Wilfongs residence in the Andalusia Apartments has been preserved in great part. The counter and splash is finished in herringbone-patterned red tiles. The Zwebells provided the room with plenty of cabinets and cutting boards to expand the counter space.

A detail of the Wilfong residence kitchen cabinets in the Andalusia Apartments displays the Spanish Revival style of the drawer pulls and cabinetry hardware.

The tile floor of the Andalusia Apartments kitchen is bordered by swirling blue-and-yellow *azulejos* and accented by decorated pavers depicting medieval themes like those seen on the imported tiles of the Casa del Herrero east garden room.

A Moorish copper-surfaced brazier with turned wood legs and a lower shelf is one which furnish Hearst's Casa Grande rear entrance hall. Both shelves could be used for coals.

A detail of the brazier from Casa Grande's rear entrance hall shows its petal form and decorative use of the nail heads that bead the brazier's border.

An imported Friarlero style armchair at Casa Grande shows the palatial seventeenth-century Spanish style of polished wood with an ornate carved stretcher and cross piece. The red velvet upholstery has been decorated with a central religious medallion and borders of geometric-patterned nail head ornament.

A vernacular style imported chair at the Casa Grande shows squared legs, leather upholstery and fringe. It is simply ornamented with finials, repetitive nail heads and a two-dimensionally decorated cross piece.

The master bedroom of the Casa del Herrero features an imported Spanish bed with the *Plateresco-Churrigueresco* treatment of a large crested form. Gessoed and painted, the headboard usually featured a medallion showing religious figures or scenes. This medallion features the Holy Family.

Barker Brothers copied the Spanish crested style for the twin beds in the guest room of the Adamson House. The headboard is painted at the scalloped borders and its central medallion is a heraldic family crest. The hanging Spanish-style lamp has a parchment shade.

An imported seventeenth-century Catalonian vanity is located in one bedroom of the Casa del Herrero. The decorative bowed shape of the table, green paint, gilding and the attached crested mirror are typical of the Baroque/*Churrigueresco* style.

During the revival period, furniture companies from the mid-west and east coast imitated Spanish styles. The Stickley Brothers Company produced green and yellow vanities that matched their bedroom suite. (The twin beds are visible in the mirror.) The trestle vanity table in a bedroom of the Casa de las Campanas features turned angled legs, shell and foliate decorated drawer, and an attached mirror. The matching chair has been reupholstered. (Also note the Spanish Revival *Mudéjar*-patterned built-in cabinet.)

Multi-drawer chests, *papallerias*, as well as *varguenos*, are common Spanish furnishing imported for Spanish Revival houses. The pair of seventeenth century *papallerias* on stands in the entrance hall of the Casa del Herrero are walnut and their ornament creates an architectural framework with tiny columns and lintels. The room is decorated with an imported Spanish door, a tile baseboard and tile floor accented with decorative tiles.

Marion Davies' bedroom suite at the Casa Grande, San Simeon, includes an imported Spanish *vargueno* with an arrangement of gilded metal interlace ornament and hardware. Central arabesque medallions decorate the lower gilded Spanish chest.

A Spanish Revival wood chest at the Adamson House is subtly carved in relief and ornamented with iron straps and clasp.

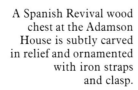

Wood benches with arches and turned wood struts were designed by the Zwebells for the Andalusia Apartments. The arches of this revival work can be compared with those of the Spanish vernacular imported chairs at Casa del Herrero.

The entrance hall of the Adamson House features a Barker Brothers Spanish Revival bench with gilded and carved decoration and wood distressed to look aged. Wrought iron supports and gilded finials add to the Spanish appearance.

The Adamson House also includes a Spanish Revival child's chair from Barker Brothers in a corner of the dining room.

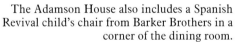

A grandfather clock in the entrance hall of the Adamson House appears like a Spanish medieval one with gilded wood carving, an iron decorated velvet front panel and a clock face crowned with finials and interlaced birds.

In William Randolph Hearst's bedroom in Casa Grande, a Spanish table is flanked by standing iron lamps with shades made from parchment sheets. Behind the lamps are Islamic panels with Arabic script in the central medallions. In 1924, Arthur Byne found the fourteenth century Spanish ceiling in a house in Tereul, and then found its frieze panels in a house in Aragon. Hearst reunited both parts for his bedroom here. Above, the frieze panels show medieval figures framed with interlace patterns.

In the Casa Grande library is an iron standing lamp with a shade made from parchment sheets from early hand-written books.

A tile-top serving cart with two shelves was used in the dining room of the Drucker House. Four tiles fitted together create each of its four medallions.

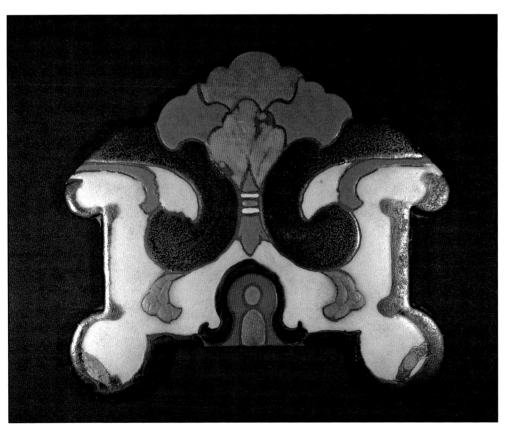

The tile border in the Adamson House entrance hall is made up of separate pieces, like this one, fitted together to create the floral motifs and shapely outline.

Parchment was used for a shade of a ceramic lamp in the entrance hall of the Adamson House. The tile-top, wrought-iron table features lighted clustered grapes and vines that decorate the apron of the table made by Malibu Potteries. The tile floor is accented with small decorative tiles and the baseboard is finished with a broad tile border.

CHAPTER FOUR

CALIFORNIA RANCH HOUSE AND HACIENDA, 1900-2000

PART ONE:
FROM RANCHO TO RANCH HOUSE

A FOLK CULTURE CASA CALIFORNIA WITH SPANISH, MEXICAN, AND NATIVE AMERICAN ROOTS

"The form called a ranch house has many roots. They go deep into the Western soil. Some feed directly on the Spanish period. Some draw upon the pioneer years. But the ranch-house growth has never been limited to its roots. It has never known a set style. It was shaped by needs for a special way of living — informal, yet gracious.

"The history of the Western ranch house is the personal history of many families — those of the soldier of Spain, the Spanish Don, the Mexican politician, the deserter from a British brig-of-war, the merchant from Boston, the fur trader, the American soldier, the adventurer, the pioneer.

"…But the greatest and most lasting influence on the blueprints brought into California was the way of living developed by the Spanish colonists."
— Cliff May, *Western Ranch Houses*, 1946

California's true multi-ethnic cultural roots surface in the California rancho hacienda and the later California ranch house where Native American, Anglo and immigrant pioneer, and Spanish and Mexican influences coalesce. While in its twentieth-century revival, California's rancho haciendas and ranch houses may be considered a part of folk culture, since they include both primitive and vernacular forms in architecture and furnishings that developed in the region's Spanish and Mexican colonial eras.

The wide variety of structural elements and decorations used for this domestic form came from California's adobes and missions, and from all types of Native American structures and simple board-and-batten or clapboard pioneer farmhouses. Most of all, the ranch house presents an idealization of the vernacular building forms that were commonplace in the Southern California landscape since its settlement.

As it has been expressed since the turn of the century, the ranch house building type also depicts the mission-to-movie lifestyle references of many Southern Californians. Regional California folk forms are a complex result of many cultures — Spanish and Mexican imports, Arts and Crafts copies, Western pioneer productions, Native American artifacts and material choices, and Anglo styles from the mid-west and New England.

Rancho Adobes and Ranch Houses, Post-1900

As early as the 1880s, there were articles about the Spanish Colonial and Mexican hacienda adobes of California and, along with the missions, many of the historic adobes of California were restored in the years after 1900. The restorations were not always based upon any historic studies of the adobe tradition, but they presented an imaginative and romantic view of what life was like.

Those interested in the adobes and California's Native population, like the advocates of the Mission Revival and members of the Arroyo culture, applied a historicist method to the indigenous architecture. Charles Lummis, who advocated preserving the missions, the adobes and the works of California's native population, believed in the Arts and Crafts principles of returning to the simple handcrafts and living close to nature. His house, with its Mission Revival elements, is unique and may be considered the earliest in the Rancho Revival. Begun in 1895, the Lummis

Despite its Mission Order gable and theoretical relationship with the Arts and Crafts movement, one of the first ranch-style houses is Charles Lummis' House, Highland Park. Built along a natural arroyo, it was rustic and meant to blend into the natural setting, as the first adobe haciendas had. Begun in 1895, Lummis continued to add personal details to the house throughout his lifetime. Today, the boulder-clad facade that the Isleta natives helped Lummis to build now faces a garden that is over-grown with mature trees.

Opposite page
A rustic setting is the ideal location for a California ranch house and Howard Arden Edwards' Antelope Valley house, 1928, is miles from others and built into the boulders of the Piute Butte. Called Swiss Chalet-style for its high-pitched roof and decorated gables, unlike a Swiss Chalet it is decorated with Native American motifs and built with local boulders. Inside, Edwards displayed his collection of California and Southwest Native American artifacts. The house was purchased and transformed into a public museum by Grace Wilcox Oliver, who added her collection to Edwards.'

house blends in with nature, especially with its arroyo boulder facade that local Isleta Indians had helped him build. The interiors also relate to nature with log ceiling beams, concrete-and-stone floors, built-in wood cabinets and shelves, and simple wood furnishings accented with straw Native American baskets.

In 1905, mission revivalist Frederick Roehrig was asked by a Chicago lawyer-turned-California esthete, Jerome Eddy, to design a house appropriate for California. Eddy, who spent his winters in Pasadena, admired Mexican houses, and Roehrig designed a tile-roofed, adobe-like house for him in brick and concrete that resembled any of the early haciendas for the land-grant Spaniards, military leaders or Mexican rancheros. Roehrig used local redwood board-and-batten paneling and ceiling beams, and local boulders for the fireplace. His design of the dining room furnishings included a built-in credenza and dining chairs assembled with wood and covered in leather with pronounced brass tacks in the Spanish manner. The house was a rare example of the adobe hacienda updated to revival standards.

Another early ranch house that expresses the uniqueness of its owner is the Antelope Valley house designed by Howard Arden Edwards in 1928-32. Edwards, a self taught artist, fell in love with the area around Piute Butte in the heart of the Mojave Desert, east of Lancaster. He homesteaded one hundred sixty acres and, with his wife and teenage son, began a house with steep angled roofs that give it a Swiss Chalet-type appearance but its exposed wood frames and gable decoration is filled with Native American motifs, and the structure incorporates large granite boulders both inside and out. Joshua trees cover the supports for its roof. Edwards filled the house with his collection of California and Southwest Native American artifacts. From the double height living room, called the Kachina Hall, a stairway leads through natural boulders to the great California Hall on the upper level, which houses thousands of artifacts, arranged as illustrated exhibits by Edwards.

In 1939, Grace Wilcox Oliver, an amateur anthropologist, discovered the Edwards house when hiking. She felt it was perfect for her own Native American collection and she persuaded Edwards to sell the property and the collection to her. The next year, she opened the house as the Antelope Valley Indian Museum and ran it for three decades. It is now a part of the California State Park System, and represents one of the largest collections of Southwestern, California and Great Basin Native American artifacts, and the structure is listed on the National Register of Historic Places.

In the 1930s, illustrated books and articles began to surface detailing the local historical examples of adobes and the Monterey Colonials, particularly Donald Hannaford and Revel Edwards' 1931 book, *Spanish Colonial or Adobe Architecture of California, 1800-1850.* Publications like this one showed that, to some extent, the followers of the Spanish Revival did show an interest in local developments — although less so than the imported European influence.

Pride in the local adobes, like the Avila Adobe in Los Angeles or the Estudillo Adobe in San Diego, gave further justification to the myth that California had experienced generations of Spanish cultural source material. However, updated versions of California's simple adobe homes didn't result from the copy book experience like that of the European Spanish styles. While some architects did render the Spanish Andalusian farmhouse types like a rancho hacienda — as Wallace Neff did for his 1924 Parker Toms Residence in San Marino— it seemed that only a few individualists, like Lummis and Edwards, and cowboy actors, like Will Rogers, Harry Carey and William S. Hart, would be inspired by the unassuming but venerable hacienda and ranch house.

Opposite page
Top: Inside the courtyard of the Avila House, a *corredor* provides access from one room to the next. The undecorated wood posts, doors and shutters are very plain and inspiring to the California Rancho Revival in the purity of their design.

Bottom: Wallace Neff's Spanish Revival Parker Toms House, San Marino, 1924, has elements of the California hacienda and ranch house, like the long, low wall, wood shutters and exposed wood lintels. The curved adobe-like wall of the exterior stair also gives the house the appearance of a Southwest style pueblo.

The Avila House, circa 1818, is the oldest house in Los Angeles and its simple, no frills style was copied during the California Rancho Revival. The front *portal* is raised from the street and has windows that can be closed with wood shutters. Plain benches furnish the *portal*.

Native American Influence of the 1900-1940 Pueblo Revival

Southern California's pueblo revival, a minor movement from approximately 1900 to 1940, added to the Rancho Revival in several key respects. First, it promoted the close-to-nature forms and materials of the local historic adobes and native culture, and second, it frequently presented designs that seemed like stage-sets or movie sets and, therefore, escapist in nature. During the Mission Revival, there were many advocates, art collectors and self-taught ethnologists and archaeologists who adopted the pueblo style of architecture to their houses.

In 1907, Irving Gill designed the Bailey Residence, La Jolla, in a flat-roof pueblo style. To house a Southwest art collection, he designed a redwood board-and-batten living room with a mezzanine bridge to the bedrooms. The home featured innovative interlocking spaces, with airy lofty areas contrasting cozy lower ones. Despite the traditional materials and the collection of rugs, pots, baskets, and Gill's own design of ranch house furniture of redwood and cowhide, the pueblo style house was very modern in architectural form.

Such pueblo-like structures had their origins in the vernacular architecture of the Southwest, now, portions of New Mexico, Arizona, Colorado and Texas. The pueblo dwellings of Native Americans and the seventeenth- and eighteenth-century Spanish settlers were handcrafted from sun-dried mud brick and rough-hewn logs, cousins to the California missions and adobes. Although the tribes of California's Native Americans never enjoyed a full-blown pueblo-type architecture, they had built some mud adobe *jacals* influenced by the Spanish mission adobes in their last remaining years before statehood and the Anglo takeover. Author Helen Hunt Jackson in her novel *Ramona* set in the early- to mid-nineteenth century, describes how the fictional characters of Ramona and Alessandro had lived in an adobe *jacal*.

The appreciation of the native crafts and way of life received a boost during the European period revivals of the 1920s and 1930s, and the pueblo saw a mild revival. Part of the interest in the style came from the same 1915 Panama-California Exposition in San Diego that spawned the European-influenced Spanish Revival. Representing New Mexico, Isaac Hamilton Rapp, who advocated the pueblo revival in Santa Fe, designed the pueblo-like New Mexico Building. Other architects in California had a preference for the modern simplicity of the pueblo, such as Irving Gill and modernist Rudolph Schindler, who designed an apartment group, the Pueblo Ribera Court, 1923, La Jolla, in the style.

In New Mexico, the native pueblo style had continued to flourish in the revivalist 1920s and 1930s, where it still exists today as the Southwest, or Santa Fe, style. As an interior design vocabulary, it has now spread to innumerable states — and countries — but works best as an architectural style in locations with dry climates and desert-like landscapes like Southern California.

The Southwest features of the pueblo revival were more refined and could be copied as motifs better than the rambling features and decorative motifs of California's original eighteenth-century adobes. The pueblo revival offered simple rectilinear design of flat-roofed, adobe brick structures. These buildings had rounded corners, simple openings, protruding beam-ends; with the walls sometimes battered and occasionally buttressed. Curved fireplaces, low parapet walls, simple carved bracket capitals over porch columns, and door and window lintels were expressed as exposed wood beams. Windows may have been casement or sash. Doors were simple boards.

The Mission Village, from 1932 in Culver City, was a motel made to look like an *Indianola* with teepees surrounding a mission style entrance gateway. The taste for native and rancho haciendas was great in the 1930s and 40s with the popularity of cowboy movies and Westerns depicting a romanticized version of the Spanish and Mexican colonial period in California.

Often, open pergola-like structures of rough-hewn logs or beams covered openings or balconies on an upper level. Floors were covered in clay tile. Ornament was seldom used, since only exposed structural elements were considered decorative. Projecting from the parapet, unpainted rough-hewn logs, or *vigas*, were typical at the roof line, as were *canales*, projecting rain water spouts.

In the 1920s-1930s, a large part of pueblo revival buildings in California were used for amusement or as a kind of commercial tourist attraction to draw visitors to hotels, motels, apartments, radio stations and movie theatres. In the Los Angeles-area, there was the Tower Auto Court, 1929, in North Hollywood, which had a pueblo-like, stepped tower at the entrance. A diner and a gas station, also at the entrance, were part of the appeal to stop at the motel.

Likewise, the Mission Village, 1932, in Culver City, was more than a tourist motel — it was a complex of buildings made to look like an original "Indianola," where post-statehood Native Americans clustered their dwellings near a rancho or pueblo. The Mission Village appeared like a Hollywood set, with a scalloped mission-style parapet at the motor court's gateway entrance where teepees were installed — although California's native population never employed the stick-and-hide conical building form.

One Southern California architect, Robert Stacy-Judd, worked predominantly in the pueblo style, an influence on the California ranch house and rancho hacienda. His Atwater Bungalows are Southwest style apartments with shapely, adobe-like walls, flat roofs, *canale* projections, and rustic wooden garage doors.

Robert Stacy-Judd was the sole Southern California architect of note producing works in the 1920s and 1930s pueblo revival. Since the architectural style and pre-Columbian decoration were Native American, he advocated that his exotic combinations were the correct architecture for America. His design of the Atwater Bungalows, 1931, Los Angeles, remains today as a romantic example of the Southwest pueblo revival apartment complex, with *viga*s projecting out of the upper portions of the walls and stick ladders leading to the upper terraces. Stacy-Judd also designed the one-story Aztec Hotel, 1925-27, in Monrovia. Despite its glass-fronted shops, it's pueblo-like in its massing, and pre-Columbian in the decorative detail, carried out in cast concrete and stucco.

The same pre-Columbian native decorations and pueblo massing were also adapted by Morgan, Walls and Clements for the Mayan Theatre, 1927, still extant in downtown Los Angeles. And as late as 1949, the pueblo style inspired the design of a church in San Fernando. Located across from an adobe, the Native American style seems quite relevant in San Fernando, where there is a nearby adobe mission.

COWBOYS AND WESTERNS

A number of cowboy actors felt the Spanish provincial-style house or rancho hacienda was appropriate for them, especially when they wanted the courtyard-type compound to include stables and riding arcas. Fred Thomson had his 1923-25 Spanish house in Beverly Hills designed by Wallace Neff, and in 1934-36, actor Francis Lederer designed his own stone, gabled horse stables. He created it in the picturesque mission style, although it was well beyond the Mission Revival period. Later, the city cut through his estate to extend Sherman Way and Lederer's wife took the opportunity to remodel the stables as a gift shop to sell Mexican and Californian crafts. The stone stables, called Canoga Mission Gallery, was also used as a community social hall and has become a regional landmark.

In the 1920s, Western actor Harry Carey also operated a crafts gallery, which he called a trading post — a simple *portal*-fronted adobe, displaying Southwest and local Native American wares — such as rugs, pots and baskets. It was located on his ranch in the Santa Clarita area, which was extremely important to many early Western movies. The rugged landscape provided the perfect setting to film cowboys riding horses and jumping the famous distance of Beale's Cut, a steep gorge. Cowboy actors and their studios also used the nearby Walt Disney Studios' frontier town, sets and herds of bison.

Carey had built a simple ranch out of adobe, including a main house, stables, guest cottages, service structures and buildings for the ranch hands. The main house was a simple Spanish hacienda with a long *portal* furnished with wagon-wheel furniture.

In 1921, cowboy star William S. Hart purchased a ranch house and surrounding property in Santa Clarita. An actor since his twenties, Hart came to Hollywood at forty-nine to start his movie career and, during the next eleven years, he made more than sixty-five silent films, becoming the leading man of the Westerns. In 1925-28, Hart commissioned architect Arthur Kelly to design a fine Spanish provincial style house for an upper ridge. He named it "La Loma de Los Vientos" and assembled a collection of Western art, Native American artifacts and early Hollywood memorabilia to furnish it.

Above: Stacy-Judd's Aztec Hotel, Monrovia, 1925-27, employs native Aztec motifs and adobe like walls.

Left: Numerous cowboy actors of the 1920s had Spanish-Mexican-Indian-Pioneer homes. Actor Harry Carey had a trading post on his ranch, located in the Santa Clarita area. It was a simple *portal*-fronted adobe, displaying Native American rugs, pots and baskets.

Below: The leading man of the Westerns, William S. Hart bought Santa Clarita property that had a simple ranch house on it. Hart used it to film movies and commissioned architect Arthur Kelly to design a Spanish Andalusian style house for him on an upper ridge. He named the two-hundred-sixty-five-acre estate Horseshoe Ranch. Hart's 1925-28 Spanish style house includes a balcony with turned balusters and bracket columns. The circular tower encloses the staircase and the three-story square tower is crowned by a cowboy weather vane.

Hart's ranch came with a 1910 board-and-batten ranch house which was used to film movies. In addition to the main house, he built a bunk house and guest house. Today, Hart's home and two-hundred-sixty-five-acre Horseshoe Ranch is open to the public as a county park. It includes an assortment of animals, including the remaining small herd of bison from Disney Studios and Hart's original board-and-batten ranch house, filled with exhibits and appearing today as it had when used as a movie set.

While cowboy actors had Spanish-Mexican-Indian-Pioneer homes of their own, movies brought the Spanish style and California ranch house into all of America's homes. Western films depicted themes of the multi-ethnic settlers of California, the Southwest and Mexico and revealed images of their structures, furniture and decorative arts.

William S. Hart's *The Squaw Man*, 1914, is considered the first major Hollywood production, and his body of work is praised for its realism, its layers of dust and mud, and the pigs and chickens that had the run of the town. Buildings were shacks, lean-tos and saloons with dirt floors. Hart's *Hell's Hinges*, 1916, was one of his best. It was about incidents in the pioneer town of Placer Centre, known as "Hell's Hinges." The major set was the Palace of Joy Saloon, which gave a crude but authentic slice of early California décor with chairs made locally of two-by-fours and imported Victorian strut-back chairs.

There were other depictions of the state, its history, its ranch houses and Spanish and American furnishings seen in the 1927 and 1947 versions of *California*, covering the history of California from the gold strike in 1848 to its admission to the union in 1850. The same themes were also covered in 1936 in *Sutter's Gold*, regarding a gold rush incident that took place just prior to California statehood, and depicting the Native American and adobe elements of *vigas* and *canales* found in the Mexican Sonoran province.

Movies and television spread the images of California's historic Spanish style and ranch houses across America. From the gold strike in 1848 to statehood in 1850, California's "Wild West" period was the subject of several films, among them was *Sutter's Gold*, 1936. It depicted a gold rush incident that took place immediately before statehood, and it showed Native American and rancho adobe structures found in Southern California and the Mexican Sonoran province.

William S. Hart's bunk house appears like a simple California Rancho Revival adobe. It is a one-story tile-roof building with a front *portal* and French doors covered with simple grills.

Films with Spanish-Mexican interiors inspired designers and owners of Spanish-style houses and California ranch houses. The 1929 film *In Old Arizona*, one of the first Cisco Kid films, was shot in Utah and based on the Spanish-Mexican character from O. Henry's story "The Caballero's Way." Some furniture from this film, particularly a chair with a rope seat detail, supposedly inspired the production of Barker Brothers' Monterey furniture when a decorator came to the Los Angeles store with a photo from the film.

In the Cisco Kid series, many sets of Spanish-Mexican design depicted a festive style of outdoor living and dining with decorative stitched tablecloths and painted wood spindle-back chairs with rush seats, as well as ornate stitched and studded costumes. Another film, *Breed of the Border*, 1933, showed rustic interiors of peeled log with Spanish *luminarias* and *vargueno* cabinets. There were other 1930s films of Mexican themes and heroes like Zorro and Pancho Villa, but by the 1940s, images of the gringo cowboy began to replace the *vaquero*. The sets for the 1941 *Riders of the Purple Sage* included Anglo farmhouses with plaid tablecloths, imported German horn chairs and Native American rugs, and fewer Spanish-Mexican references.

By the 1950s, the stories of Cisco Kid and Zorro were made into weekly television shows. However, they were seen along with gringos like the Lone Ranger, Roy Rogers and Gabby Hayes, and films also were decidedly becoming all-American. The Western hit of 1953 was *Shane*, and its important interior was a peeled log bar — a classic hunting lodge décor — set in the Grand Tetons of Wyoming and Utah. Also, the early American sets of the 1954 *Bad Day at Black Rock* showed a saloon full of the curved-back "western" chairs that would soon furnish many Midwestern dens. One of the last great Westerns, the 1957 *Gunfight at the OK Corral*, set in Tombstone, Arizona, however, shows a multi-ethnic setting similar to California's true pioneer towns, with a Spanish adobe church juxtaposed with plain board-and-batten structures and simple wooden barns.

In general, the pattern of Westerns in film and television seemed to parallel the development of the California rancho. Sets, like the ranchos, evolved from the romantic and florid Spanish-Mexican style to the simpler, straightforward, all-American Anglo-pioneer style — finally creating a combination of the two, along with the inclusion of Native American stick-and-hide furnishings and artifacts.

Breed of the Border, 1933, displayed rustic interiors of peeled log with Spanish *luminarias* and *vargueno* cabinets. In addition, the *Cisco Kid* series, featured Spanish-Mexican sets and other 1930s films featured Hispanic heroes like Zorro and Pancho Villa. However, by the 1940s, images of the gringo cowboy began to replace the *vaquero*, and by the 1950s, the Cisco Kid and Zorro were on weekly television shows, along with gringo heroes like the Lone Ranger and Roy Rogers.

PIONEER INFLUENCE ON THE CALIFORNIA RANCH HOUSE

Throughout the nineteenth century, Anglo settlers of many European backgrounds built simple, unaffected rural styles, constructing plain clapboard and board-and-batten farm houses. The houses were not usually worthy of study until renowned characters and rugged individualists like Will Rogers, "The Cherokee Kid," began to build and decorate their houses with elements celebrating the multi-ethnic settlement of Southern California.

Born in Oogolah Indian territory in 1879 to parents of Cherokee blood, Will Rogers became a cowboy entertainer, homespun philosopher and American ambassador of good will. Rogers loved his acreage, polo field and simple ranch house in Pacific Palisades, as well as his life of churning out news columns and riding and roping with the likes of Spencer Tracy, Clark Gable and Daryl Zanuck.

As a young man, Rogers worked as a cowhand on his father's Oklahoma ranch. He then began traveling, first to Argentina and later to South Africa, where he perfected his rope act in Texas Jack's Wild West Circus. In 1916, he was recruited by the Ziegfeld Follies to add humor to the show, and there Rogers began skewering politicians regarding events of World War I. In 1919, Samuel Goldwyn invited him to Hollywood, where his role in a few talkies gave him the name of the "Cowboy Philosopher."

Perhaps the name that fits Rogers best was the one he received when his roping days brought him to New Zealand. Called "The Mexican Rope Artist," Rogers appreciated the roping skill he first learned, not in Mexico, but in South America. He also appreciated the crafts of the many cultures he encountered in his travels and in his adopted home of Southern California.

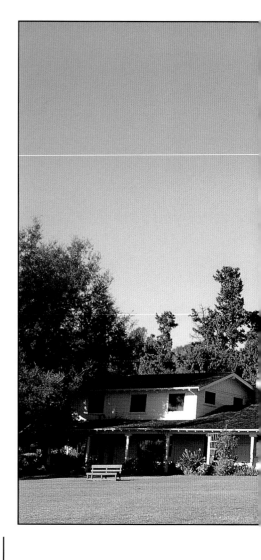

In 1927, Will Rogers directed construction of a six-room cabin northwest of his polo field. The building was designed as a weekend retreat by architect A.C. Semrow, and built under the direction of Rogers' brother-in-law, Lee Adamson. It was a white board-and-batten "box" house, with a green roof and a wide porch across the front. The interior contained a kitchen, three bedrooms, a bath, and a large living room with a fireplace made of stones from the property.

The two-story guest house southwest of the ranch house was built in 1928, and designed by architect E. Sprout and its board-and-batten structure matched the original ranch cabin in color and style. In 1929, Rogers and his family moved permanently to the ranch and, using pictures of a Montana ranch house Rogers had visited, he asked architect Ken Reese to design a comfortable, unpretentious addition. The young architect, working for the Beverly Hills architectural firm of Asa Hudson, drew up plans for a 13-room addition to be located north of the cabin. This wing contained a small sitting room, a sewing room, a study for Rogers, a master bedroom, a bedroom for each of the three children, a guest room, and servants' quarters that connected southward to the original kitchen. With the new private family quarters to the north, the original cabin, or south wing, was used for entertaining and for meals when bad weather forced the family indoors off the courtyard, where Rogers preferred to dine.

In 1931 and 1935, further alterations and additions were made, one allowed for a greater number of guest rooms, and another created a stair off of Rogers' upstairs study, allowing him to come and go unnoticed by company. The last major changes had taken place only a few months before Rogers died unexpectedly in an airplane crash. The main house is now a two-story wooden building, with wings connected by servant quarters and a courtyard.

Opposite page
The porch of Will Rogers' original cabin shows that the house was what he asked for, "a white board-and-batten 'box' house with ...a wide porch across the front." The north addition is located just beyond the dining patio with its pergola linking the original porch to the one of the addition. Although the wood materials and decorative wood scallop appear like elements of an Anglo farmhouse, the feeling of the porch is like that of a Spanish or Mexican hacienda of old California.

Will Rogers' Pacific Palisades house is a fine example of a California Ranch House. Clad in common Anglo pioneer materials — board-and-batten and clapboard — the house sprawls across the lawn above Rogers' polo field. In 1927, the first six-room cabin (left half of photograph) was built as the Rogers' vacation home by architect A.C. Semrow. The family moved permanently to the ranch in 1929 and added a 13-room addition north of the cabin and separated by a dining patio (right half of photograph). The addition was inspired by a Montana ranch house and designed by Ken Reese of Asa Hudson's architectural firm. Inside, Spanish Revival and Native American furnishings pay respect to California's colonial past.

The original cabin best displays the original furnishings and artwork of the Rogers family. In the dining area, the table and chairs of stenciled pigskin-and-willow are Mexican Equipale pieces given to Rogers as a gift by a Mexican governor of Jalisco. Around the grand boulder fireplace are other major pieces that were part of their collection of "Monterey" furniture in the living-dining room, Rogers' study and family bedrooms. The pieces were purchased at Barker Brothers, which commissioned the designs made by Mason Furniture Company of Los Angeles.

In addition, Rogers had accumulated a collection of Native American rugs and Western artifacts, as well as international gifts given to him and his family over the years by admirers. Rogers' collection of paintings, prints and sculptures is comprised of the work of early twentieth-century Western artists, some of whom were personal friends of Rogers, like Ed Borein and Charles Russell.

Rogers had decided to make one structural change to the original cabin, while his wife, Betty, was touring Israel. When Betty called home, he told her he was "just raising the roof." Later, he wrote in his column that perhaps Betty was right when she said he remodeled "just so he could rope in the house without hitting the ceiling." The enlarged space gave Rogers plenty of room to keep up his skill in Mexican rope tricks. Rogers kept a bucket of ropes beneath the living room stairs, and when he had guests, he would pull the ropes out and perform his lassoing tricks on them. Friend and cowboy artist Ed Borein, tired of being roped, gave Rogers a stuffed calf on which to practice his roping skills.

While the Rogers house appears like a plain American farmhouse, its interiors — particularly those of the original cabin — reflect the evolution of California's Spanish and Mexican colonial styles.

Part Cherokee Indian, Will Rogers furnished the wood paneled living-dining room of the original six-room cabin with numerous Native American blankets and rugs. Before the fireplace are silhouetted cowboy andirons, and a barrel of ropes at the foot of the stair allowed Rogers to perform his cowboy lassoing tricks on his guests. The animal heads were gifts and the swing came from the Rogers' Beverly Hills home.

A narrow mezzanine gallery overlooks the Rogers living-dining room. Leading to the mezzanine and the bedrooms is a stair made from railroad ties. Rogers opened the ceiling of this section of the cabin to perform his rope tricks in the house without hitting the ceiling. Rogers' friend, cowboy artist Ed Borein, gave him the stuffed calf to practice his roping. The earless calf shows it was well-used.

CLIFF MAY AND THE CALIFORNIA RANCH HOUSE

The Will Rogers House, relaxed yet added onto as needed, was the kind of structure in which builder-architect Cliff May found inspiration and dubbed the "California ranch house" in his 1946 book, *Western Ranch Houses*. May was an advocate of this style, although it was more of a vernacular form than a style, and its designers and architects were less known, or unknown. A former builder from San Diego, May defined the contemporary California ranch house in his book and in his own work, inspired by the adobes and pioneer houses of California and haciendas of Mexico.

The text of May's 1946 book was brief, but its messages and images were influential across America, and the publication went into repeated printings. Significantly, May pointed out that the California ranch style was identifiable from the 1920s. He wrote:

"We think that it was these ranch houses that Henry H. Saylor, editor of *The American Architect*, was thinking about when, in 1925, he wrote this paragraph in an article reviewing fifteen years of home building on the Pacific Coast:

'There was still another type that stood out from the medley of jumbled styles, lack of styles, or mere affectations, and that was the California ranch house. It never put forth any great claims of merit, it never really entered the lists to establish itself as the vogue… [I]t never laid claim even to a name, and yet there it stands, a vernacular that is as unmistakably a part of its California foothills as the stone houses of eastern Pennsylvania betoken that great treasure store of mica schist. Unfortunately, there were few of these ranch houses compared with the multitude of suburban bungalows, and they were usually well off the beaten track where their quiet influence could have little effect on public taste.'"

May describes many aspects he appreciated in buildings from the 1830s, such as

Cliff May's early designs in the San Diego area, included a 1936 house, which hugged the natural form of a low hill. It featured a tile roof, wood shutters and wood straight spindle grills. May, a builder and self-trained architect, was inspired by Southern California's adobes and ranch houses and he coined the term "California Ranch House" in his 1946 book, *Western Ranch Houses*. May wrote about adobe buildings from the 1830s with porches, low roofs, *corredors*, patios, and close-to-the-ground effects. Although the California Ranch House has so many variations and is still considered more of a vernacular form than a style, May's works and writings did much to make it known across America.

the porch, the low roof, the *corredor*, the patio, and the close-to-the-ground effect of the adobes. He also claimed that Monterey-type houses were built everywhere in California prior to the appearance of that type in Monterey. He pointed to — among others — Don Bernardo Yorba's adobe on Rancho Santa Ana, 1835, which had a large patio, and on two sides, the building was two stories high with balconies.

May's Commodore Seligmann residence, 1935-36, on the Coronado Peninsula, was very much like a California adobe, with whitewashed stucco walls, red tile roof and courtyards. The interior ceilings were defined with *vigas* and *latias*, but the fireplaces were produced in painted wood with carpentry that appeared to be inspired by New England designs.

May's early designs in the San Diego area, included the Trenchard House, circa 1936, which hugs the natural form of the low hill and it featured a low angle tile roof, wood shutters and straight wood spindle grills. The motor court was designed as a private courtyard with a doorway and garage doors patterned in a strigil pattern, a simple swirl derived from classical and neoclassical decorative objects that is a form found on mission gates and doors and in Spanish Revival houses. Nearby, another 1930s ranch house by May appears like a California adobe hacienda with few openings on its front wall, only a wood grill over one set of windows and chevron-patterned entrance gates.

May appreciated the work of a contemporary, William Wurster, an architect in Northern California, and particularly praised his 1927 Gregory Ranch, comprised of gable-roofed, board-and-batten buildings with stables in a rancho compound located in the Santa Cruz Mountains. Adopting the board-and-batten material of Wurster's design and Will Rogers' cabins, May's own home, Mandalay, 1951-80, Brentwood, nonetheless expressed the low, one-story, close-to-the-earth effects of houses made of adobe. May continued to add onto his own home for decades, and he designed a number of other houses in the Mandeville Canyon area of Los Angeles in the same manner, detailing them with Spanish and Mexican features, imported architectural elements and furnishings.

Another San Diego area house by Cliff May appears like a California adobe hacienda with few openings on its front wall. Only a straight spindle grill over high-set windows, chevron-patterned entrance gates and a low tile roof accent the adobe-like wall. In May's 1946 book, he pointed out that the California Ranch House style was identifiable from the 1920s and he noted: "We think that it was these ranch houses that Henry H. Saylor, editor of *The American Architect*, was thinking about when, in 1925, he wrote: 'There was still another type that stood out from the medley of jumbled styles, lack of styles, or mere affectations, and that was the California ranch house...a vernacular that is... unmistakably a part of its California foothills...'"

CONTEMPORARY RANCHO REVIVAL: CALIFORNIA HACIENDAS AND RANCH HOUSES, 1970-2000

There are many California ranch house masterpieces from the last quarter of the century since many architects, designers and collectors have come to appreciate the works of both the Spanish Colonial Revival and the Rancho Revival movements and recognize the theoretical relationship between the two.

Regarding the ranch house or hacienda, as typical of modern influences on many period styles after the 1950s and 1960s, some architects dramatized and exaggerated the shapes and angles of the typical California ranch house. Cliff May did this for his Axline Residence, 1978-81, Rancho Santa Fe. It is a masterful extension of the courtyard plan home with the traditional angled roofline attenuated and the walls made to look adobe-like. On the interiors, white-washed *latias* and *vigas* accent the angled ceilings and large white *saltillos* surface the floors. The room size is extremely spacious and, like May's own Mandalay, the house is decorated with Mexican and Spanish doors, grills and decorative artifacts.

In these last three decades, May and others furnish their haciendas, casas, and ranch houses with pieces from a grand mix of Hispanic and Anglo cultures. Such items include Mexican "rustico" reproduction furniture, which use old wood and pieces from authentic Mexican antiques. Other Mexican pieces include reproduction chests, *roperos* (armoires) and *trasteros* (tall cabinets with turned spindle doors). These pieces might be made of mesquite or *sabino*, a golden Mexican cypress, and they are frequently decorated with scratch-and-gouge carvings that give an aged appearance and create crude vernacular interpretations of motifs. Some of these same classic Spanish-Mexican furniture forms may have been retrieved as antiques from the colonial Southwest, particularly from around Santa Fe, New Mexico.

Also, Indiana's Hickory furniture would fit well in these interiors with their simple wood frames and cane woven chair seats, since cane and rush seats were common to both Spanish and rancho furniture. Hickory Furniture had a presence in California and it furnished a hotel on Catalina. Additionally, Gustav Stickley's Arts and Crafts "Mission" pieces were collected for these houses, along with copper-and-mica lamps from the first part of the century that had been produced by San Francisco-area craftsmen at The Palmer Copper Shop and Old Mission Kopper Kraft. The best known, and most collected, lamps were those by Dirk Van Erp, produced at his Copper Shop.

A California ranch house or hacienda often included such novelty items as horn furniture since it went well with other primitive Native American furnishings or artifacts made of unaltered natural materials. Horn furniture had been popular in Texas at the turn of the century and was originally an English and German furniture type for hunting lodges. Its use in California ranch houses made these rustic allusions while fitting in with other rustic furnishings, including horn chandeliers and sconces.

Ramada-like cantina pavilions were frequently added to the rear facades of ranch houses to create Western style terraces, and interiors could be decorated to exaggerate Western "cowboy" elements. Furnishings would include wagon-wheels used for chandeliers and "arms" of sofas and benches, barrels made into chairs, and cowboy silhouetted weathervanes and fireplace screens.

Of unique interest had been collecting works by, or inspired by, Thomas Molesworth. His furniture produced in Cody, Wyoming was one of the first to base a high style on a rustic vernacular furniture type. Molesworth's peeled log, tree-limb and burled-wood pieces could be seen at large hotels in Wyoming and Montana. They had gained attention from these hotel commissions, as well as their reputation for furnishing the Rockefellers' Jackson Hole, Wyoming home and President Eisenhower's Gettysburg, Pennsylvania home. Molesworth's work included sheepskin lampshades and fireplace screens with silhouettes of cowboys, saddles and longhorn cattle. Also, the primitive-based materials and cowboy images were easily copied by Californians for their contemporary ranch houses.

Regarding the Spanish Revival, Southern California's cultural fusion approach accounts for such comfortable designs as the Culberg Residence, a 1928 Spanish Colonial Revival hunting lodge in the hills above Malibu, rebuilt after a fire by architect Carl Day, and completed with a pool house and landscaping by Doug and Regula Campbell in 1992. A stone tower, stone fireplaces, an enclosed courtyard and a bunkhouse-style pool house makes the hacienda-style hunting lodge a suitable home for a collection of Hickory and early California furniture.

Likewise, a 1920s Los Angeles bungalow remodeled in 1986 by resident/designer Thomas Callaway and architect James Chuda presents an ethnic mix of Spanish, Native American, Mexican and Anglo elements that could be found during the original Spanish colonial period. Adobe-like walls and eighteenth-century Argentine ironwood window frames and grills give the house an aura of age. The interiors are tasteful juxtapositions of high culture and peasant taste with imported antiques and Native American and Western artifacts. Like nineteenth-century settlers, the Callaways decorated the interiors with an eclectic mix of European heirlooms, Native American artifacts, Spanish-Mexican imports and local furnishings.

The recent Spanish Revival Ventura ranch house of Joel Shukowsky as well as Diane Keaton's former Beverly Hills Wallace Neff house (with its Monterey furniture) perpetuate the combination of Spanish Revival style with California ranch house elements with great sophistication. On the other hand, in Santa Barbara, architect Thomas Bollay is repeating the forms of 1920s Spanish revivalist George Washington Smith and Joseph Plunkett with modern planning and contemporary amenities. His own home reflects this current "revival" of the Spanish Revival and its facade is hardly distinguishable from the reserved type of Smith's Osthoff House in San Marino. Bollay's house is furnished with many Spanish Revival pieces, such as a 1920s-30s dining table and chairs by the Los Angeles Furniture Company that could have been based on such imported pieces as found in the Casa del Herrero.

A great number of other designers and architects, particularly Douglas Burdge of Malibu, produce fine Southern California versions of the Spanish-Mexican hacienda. Although calling these comfortable houses "hacienda style," they have a greater high style appearance rather than the rustic folk art allusions of the California rancho hacienda. For example, Burdge's courtyard houses include such Spanish Revival decorative detail as rich tile walls, stone work window- and door-surrounds, and quatrefoil windows, as well as other metal, stone and wood details. Burdge is educated in California's historic architecture and his inclusion of imported Mexican architectural elements and furniture is a conscious blend of the casual and the formal. Although these houses are well-based in their Mexican sources, they show an understanding that building for Southern California's climate, landscape and historic past return us again to the educated goals of 1920s Spanish Colonial revivalists.

PART TWO

EXTERIOR AND INTERIOR DETAILS OF THE CALIFORNIA RANCH HOUSE AND HACIENDA

ENTRANCES, GATES,
PAVING AND SURFACING

Courtyards are predominant elements of the California Ranch House since the style promotes living out of doors. One of Cliff May's ranch houses near San Diego uses a brick-paved courtyard as a motor court. For privacy, a gate, right, separates it from the street and a recessed wood door leads to an inner courtyard. A simple lintel over the door and the plain, straight spindled grill over the window, right, are reminiscent of the humble adobes built by California's earliest pioneers. Entrance gates, door and garage doors are decorated with a strigil form, a simple swirl, that is found on mission gates and on Spanish Revival garden gates.

An iron bell announces guests to the Korpinen-Ericson Hacienda in Palm Springs, where a tall redwood fence overgrown with hedges hides the courtyard. Flagstone-and-concrete walkways lead past a Mexican tiered fountain to the wide entrance *portal*. Furnishings of the early 1930s Spanish-style ranch house are introduced on the *portal* with its iron chandelier and pair of standing *luminarias* beside the double entrance doors.

Ranch houses tend to use natural materials in unaltered form — an influence of Native American life — and a twig fence surrounding the garden of a Montectio house show this material preference applied to garden fences of both Spanish and Rancho Revival houses.

Pounded earth is a common courtyard surface treatment for a ranch house. It is used at the entrance to the Lummis House, Los Angeles, and throughout its garden paths.

The rear courtyard of the Lummis House is also surfaced in pounded earth. The simple dirt is accented with arroyo stone borders around some of the plantings, and around the aged sycamore tree for which the house is named, "El Alisail." The back of the house is finished in stucco and features a covered porch upheld by straight wood posts.

THE ONE-ROOM CABIN

Left: The rear courtyard of the Lummis House is enclosed by a ring of tiny cabins that are scarcely larger than one room. The charismatic Lummis always had friends show up from foreign countries and from across America. Appearing like a rancho compound with bunk houses or service buildings, Lummis' concrete guest houses appear adobe-like with curved walls and wooden porches and doors.

Bottom left: Will Rogers' Pacific Palisades house gives the feeling of being a one-room cabin in its large living-dining room. The open gable ceiling embracing the large living space adds to this character. The design was inspired by simple ranch house and farmhouse structures that were seldom larger than one room. Here, in addition to Rogers' collection of Native American rugs and Western artifacts, there are numerous paintings, prints and sculptures by early twentieth-century Western artists, like Ed Borein and Charles Russell, who were Rogers' personal friends.

Bottom right: The living room is so important to the Korpinen-Ericson Hacienda that — like early California haciendas — it feels like a one-room cabin. Dining can take place at the wrought iron tables on the wide *portal*, while living is accommodated in the cozy, gable-ceiling space. Above the entrance doors, completely open to the *portal*, is a decorative border that seems to be inspired by the Native American work at Mission churches. The sofa, chair, standing lamp, stool, writing desk and chair are pieces of Monterey furniture produced by Barker Brothers.

FIREPLACES

There is a unique fireplace at one end of the large double-height room that Lummis called his "*museo*." Inspired by native cultures, Lummis hardly altered the natural materials he used to build it. Two peeled logs support three wood shelves and a hollowed out log creates a central ornament – a small cabinet latched with an iron clasp. The logs are protected from the heat of the hearth by hammered copper sheets. To the right is a paneled door to the dining room made of hand-hewn wood by Lummis. Appearing as plain as the pounded earth courtyards, Lummis' interior ground floor rooms are surfaced in concrete.

The large fireplace of the Rogers House is made of stones taken from the property and its rustic appearance goes well with the rough-sawn cedar boards of the walls. All the comfortable seating is arranged around the hearth, including three Monterey chairs (two dark "Old Wood" and one "Spanish Red"). Matching the suspended swing is a green "Spanish Moss" Monterey sofa with an attached table, foreground.

Palos Verdes stone forms the outdoor fireplace used to warm the Rogers' patio. Shaded during a part of the day by an adjacent pergola, the patio was the primary dining location for the Rogers family. (When barbecuing took place, pits were placed out on the adjacent lawn.) The railroad tie stairs with iron stair rail led upstairs to one son's bedroom. A simple lantern lights the space under the balcony.

The stone fireplace in the Korpinen-Ericson Hacienda, Palm Springs, has a wood mantle that matches the light color of the gable ceiling. A framed Catalina tile bird plaque decorates the over-mantle and large Gladding McBean pots are placed beside the hearth. The dark "Old Wood" Monterey sofa, foreground, is accompanied with a "Straw Ivory" Monterey bench, left, decorated with flowers, and a late "Early American" style Monterey chair, right, with side wings. Decorative painting crowns the two draped entrances to the dining room and the iron drapery rods are finished with scrolls The copper-top table and tile top table date from the 1930s.

Relief tiles by Arts and Crafts craftsman Ernest Batchelder surround the hearth of Maxine Gray's small cottage in Los Angeles. Designed as a type of California ranch house, the fireplace is accented with cowboy andirons, and one of Mrs. Gray's collection of early California paintings hangs above it. A corner Monterey cupboard with iron straps and hinges is joined with other dark "Old Wood" Monterey furnishings — a chair and low table. The Monterey standing lamp of wood and wrought iron features a painted parchment shade.

The California ranch house represents individuality and one bedroom fireplace in the Lummis' House was sculpted with relief figures by Lummis' friend, the sculptor Gutzon Borglum, who carved the presidents' faces on Mount Rushmore. The mantle is finished with a Spanish blessing and a line up of carved faces Lummis collected in South America.

INTERIOR DETAILS AND BUILT-INS

The double doors between the Lummis House entrance hall and the *"museo"* are wood. The upper panels have square openings and simple geometric inlaid and incised decoration, designed and crafted by Lummis.

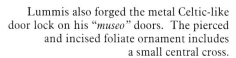

Lummis also forged the metal Celtic-like door lock on his *"museo"* doors. The pierced and incised foliate ornament includes a small central cross.

Left: Unique and personal details are built into California ranch houses. The dining room of the Lummis House features a small semi-circular niche and a small built-in wood cabinet with doors decorated with random patterned panels and upper open shelves. The niche is finished with a beamed ceiling and recessed windows that vary in scale and height. The dining room is surfaced with a concrete floor scored to look like tiles and it is furnished with Monterey-like chairs with leather seats.

Bottom left: Horse head capitals in the living-dining room of the Will Rogers ranch house were carved for the house by A. C. Semrow who designed the original cabin.

Bottom right: Built-in cabinets in the Lummis House differ in every instance and one dining room cabinet features a central window that opens to a view of the rear porch. A hanging shelf becomes the top of the built-in cabinet. Lummis was influenced by Native American designs for the small wall niches and the zigzag patterns of the upper cabinet doors.

FURNITURE — IMPORTS AND REVIVAL CREATIONS

The California ranch house accommodates an eclectic mix of European antiques, Anglo colonial furniture, Native American artifacts, Mexican and Spanish furniture. Among imports is the Spanish trestle table at the Antelope Valley ranch house of Howard Edwards, maintained for decades as a museum by Grace Wilcox Oliver. The table displays a selection of Native American baskets and below it is a Native American rug.

The Mexican Equipale furniture in the dining area of the Will Rogers House is an unusual example of the popular round pigskin-and-willow pieces found in many contemporary ranch houses. Rogers' pieces were gifts of a Mexican governor of Jalisco, and they are tooled and stenciled in pre-Columbian motifs.

The top of Rogers' Equipale table folds upward and transforms into a high-back chair.

A 1930s ad for El Rancherito Lullaby Baby Furniture shows that Spanish style rancho furniture gained popularity among manufacturers following the rise of the Spanish Revival and Rancho Revival architectural movements. Ranch style furniture appeared common and plain and few manufacturers labeled each piece with brand names, often making it difficult to trace the maker of a specific work.

On the east coast, the Arts and Crafts Stickley family — known for their oak "Mission" furniture — also got into the production of ranch style furniture as seen in this Stickley Brothers 1930s ad for "Fiesta" style pieces. Both Spanish and Ranch style lines of furniture were inspired by the California movements and were frequently made by mid-west and east coast companies.

The Antelope Valley house of Howard Edwards was furnished with a 1930s Spanish Revival *vargueno* that is placed on a table with angled spindle legs and simple vernacular style metal hardware. (Compare the *vargueno* to high style imported examples at the Casa del Herrero and Casa Grande, San Simeon.)

Fiesta style writing desk and matching chair is located in one corner of the Antelope Valley house just beyond a peeled log post. The furniture interprets the Spanish style metal hardware straps and hinges in wood. Some Native American pieces collected by Howard Edwards and Grace Wilcox Oliver are placed on the shelves.

Two common ranch style chairs at the Antelope Valley house display a "cowboy Western" appearance. The chair, left, has splayed legs and a curved hand-hold in its angled back. The chair, right, is stained orange and its slat back presents the same jaunty angle of the adjacent chair.

The doors of the Spanish Revival *vargueno* at the Antelope Valley house open and reveal a panel decorated with a Spanish galleon that folds down to become a writing surface.

MONTEREY FURNITURE

In 1929, Barker Brothers' store decorator Fred Nason brought a still photograph from a movie to Frank Mason and Louis Schmenger, owners of Mason Furniture Company of Los Angeles, to produce furniture based on the movie set. In a short time, Frank Mason and his son George designed the pieces which Barker Brothers advertised as "furniture of the Spanish Dons" and named after Monterey, the capital of the California region when it was a Spanish and Mexican colony.

The photo of the movie set was likely from *In Old Arizona*, a 1929 Cisco Kid movie that included a rustic chair with rope details at the seat. Therefore, rope details accompanied the first Monterey pieces that gave the plain Oregon alder wood works a crude rancho appearance. On the other hand, the Masons' first designs also adapted Spanish wrought iron elements and German immigrants Max Gebhart and his brothers produced the distinctive ironwork that would have been seen on imported Spanish seventeenth and eighteenth century furniture.

Barker Brothers' Monterey line was immediately popular. Western cowboy stars and celebrities bought the pieces, such as Gene Autry, Roy Rogers, Charles Bickford, Bella Lugosi, Clark Gable and Walt Disney. Will Rogers used many of the early "Classic" pieces in his home, including the dark Old Wood chair, Spanish Green sofa and Old Red chair now found around the boulder fireplace and a Straw Ivory chair and sofa in the living area. Barker Brothers also produced an unusually long tile top credenza in dark Old Wood for Rogers' dining area.

In addition to sofas, chairs, chests, dining tables and beds, the Mason Furniture Company also designed Mexican sarape-style upholstery and bedspreads, and floor lamps and table lamps that combined wood and wrought iron features. They produced some rare items like library tables, tile top tables and chests, as well as radio cabinets and baby grand pianos that were never listed in catalogs. For tile top pieces, Monterey bought tiles from Malibu Potteries, Hispanic Tile Company and Taylor Tile.

The periods of Monterey furniture have been categorized by historian and antiques dealer, Don Shorts, who is based in Ventura and runs The Old California Store. The first Classic phase, 1929-35, is the most prized and it presents prominent ironwork, such as hinges, handles, latches, strappings, and structural elements, as well as the exposed rope supports for cushions. It came in a dark wood stain (Old Wood) or stained and wiped colors (Spanish Green, Old Red, Spanish Blue and Straw Ivory) to give an antiqued appearance. Blue pieces were only made for bedroom furniture and fewer pieces were produced in green and red.

The next phase was the Orange period, from 1935 to 1938. Orange was a popular color in pottery and tile at the time, and Monterey added it to its choices. The color was used on the wood, the hinges, latches and other ironwork – although it was much muted by the antiquing stain. As the Western desert aspects became more pronounced during this phase, another color, Desert Dust, was introduced. It was similar to Straw Ivory but had a golden tone. The dry-desert effect of a crackling finish was also added during this phase and the pieces included floral decorations painted by Juan Intenoche, who later worked for Disney Animation.

The 1937-40 Western phase dropped the wrought iron features that originally made Monterey so distinguished and related it to the Spanish Revival. Thoroughly a rancho or ranch house furniture type by this date, Monterey Furniture Company introduced pieces trimmed in leather embossed with flowers like western saddles, and

painted decorations including images of cowboys, saddles, boots, donkeys, sleeping Mexicans and cactus.

In the last 1939 to 1943 Early American phase, Anglo farmhouse elements were added to the line, such as wing back chairs and sofas and Early American trestle tables. The furniture was stained brown-orange to make the alder wood appear like maple.

The early pieces had the signature stamp of a horseshoe branded into them until it became a fire hazard. Some horseshoe stamps are accompanied by the name Monterey. During World War II manufacturing ended and the company was sold in 1945.

A small side table in red at the Korpinen-Ericson Hacienda copies some of the characteristics of the popular Monterey furniture produced by Barker Brothers. It is accompanied by sleeping Mexican bookends, a tiny Native American basket and a brass cowboy hat used as an ashtray. The watercolor represents a Western cowboy who looks like the young William S. Hart.

A late "Desert Dust" Monterey style painted chest-of-drawers in the Antelope Valley house is decorated with floral painting and hardy wrought iron pulls.

Beyond a Monterey sofa, the dining table, chairs and credenza — also Monterey pieces — are located in Maxine Gray's dining room, adding to the residence's rancho revival character. The dining chairs derive their form from Spanish chairs with cresting and decorative backs with vertical spindles. (Compare with Casa del Herrero's breakfast room chairs.) Mrs. Gray recovered the sofa with Mexican style sarape upholstery.

The Monterey dining suite rendered in Straw Ivory at the Korpinen-Ericson Hacienda where the table, chairs and credenza are painted with floral motifs by Juan Intenoche. The wagon wheel is a common motif and element used to decorate ranch revival homes and at the Korpinen-Ericson Hacienda, two wagon wheels form a hanging chandelier made complete with red farmhouse lanterns. Lanterns of the Spanish-Moorish type inspired the wall sconce, left. Above the credenza is a Mexican painting on velvet and colorful Mexican pottery.

Top right: The breakfast nook of the Korpinen-Ericson Hacienda features green Monterey pieces — a square table, side chairs with leather seats, and a side table with an apron decorated with floral motifs. Tonaláware dinnerware is set on a Mexican tablecloth and Mexican plates decorate the top of the wall above a bay window.

Bottom right: Will Rogers' Monterey dining table and chairs are stained in the classic Old Wood style. The large table has a wood and metal trestle and splayed spindle legs. The side chairs are covered with leather seats and backs held by brass nail heads. The armchair has cross bars at its base.

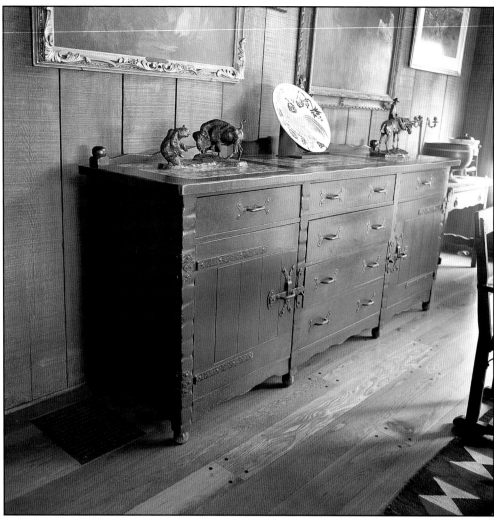

The custom-made Rogers' tile-topped Monterey credenza in the Old Wood style is almost ten feet long and organized in three sections with side cabinets and center drawers.

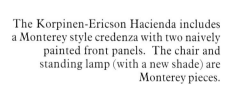

The Korpinen-Ericson Hacienda includes a Monterey style credenza with two naively painted front panels. The chair and standing lamp (with a new shade) are Monterey pieces.

A tile-top Old Wood Monterey credenza features a scalloped splashboard and metal side handles to move the piece.

A Spanish Green Monterey credenza displays the antiqued treatment of the surfaces and the flowers painted by Juan Intenoche. The cabinet doors feature a scalloped border.

For the bedroom, Monterey made chest of drawers and vanity mirrors. Those in Straw Ivory at the Korpinen-Ericson Hacienda are accompanied by a petite straw Monterey lamp and a stool.

The Korpinen Hacienda also features an Old Wood Monterey chair, a leather-covered stool and a desk that opens to provide writing space.

Another bedroom at the Korpinen-Ericson Hacienda is furnished with Old Wood Monterey bedroom furniture, including a double bed, chest of drawers and two vanity mirrors — one above the chest and one in the vanity alcove.

Barker Brothers also produced a small number of Monterey radio cabinets. This version features splayed, turned legs and a tile top. The speakers were covered by quatrefoil moldings over the cloth-covered speaker.

Maxine Gray purchased one of the rare Monterey baby grand pianos painted in Spanish Green. It features the same kind of flat curved legs as on Monterey dining tables and a scroll metal bar on the underside. The matching bench is also decorated with Juan Intenoche's flowers.

ACCESSORIES

An array of 1920s to 1940s tile-toped metal tables from the Korpinen-Ericson Hacienda is displayed in the entrance courtyard. One in the background features scroll brackets to hold two potted plants and the round one on the right was made from a 1920s car tire rim. Tile patterns vary from plain colors to geometric and floral ones to medieval crests, and the tables reflect stylistic tendencies that range from Spanish to Western and Moderne.

The California ranch house of the 1930s and 1940s would be decorated with playful tourist items gotten from nearby Mexico. A green Monterey book shelf decorated with flowers is the backdrop for a collection of straw, wood and ceramic toys and dolls of Mexican, Spanish and pioneer themes. On the wall is a painted tin figure of a Mexican on a burro. The assemblage includes working carts — one filled with a collection of copper sombreros — and pioneer covered wagons. Large and small donkeys and a carved wood donkey join pairs of dark-skinned Mexican youth with lively faces and huge round eyes.

Tin serving trays depict tranquil scenes of Mexican life. The large tray, left, is incised and tooled to create a relief scene of a bent working figure amidst hills, fields and cactus; a flat roof pueblo is located on the left. The other tray, right, is painted, depicting a sleeping Mexican, cactus and hills among which are a domed church and an adobe, red roof home. The crackled paint, wood and rope circular tray with a figure of a Mexican and cart is a Monterey work painted by Juan Intenoche.

Among ceramic and wood Mexican figures are bookends depicting pairs of seated, sleeping sombrero-clad couples. The side table is a green Monterey piece with iron hinges and trestle.

TILE AND POTTERY

California ceramic companies produced the same tourist themes gotten from Mexico. Brayton-Laguna Pottery, 1927-68, made caricatured figures of stooped Mexican men with large heads, short legs and long arms and wearing beards and sombreros. They would generally be sold as a pair with donkeys or burros, similarly rendered in a caricature mode.

Tiles also produced figures of proud Mexican *vaqueros* riding in the rugged desert setting, and sleeping Mexicans in various poses. These tiles were produced by Brayton-Laguna, whose signature tile represents their shop once located on the Pacific Coast Highway in Laguna.

A 1930s "Caballero on Horse" tile mural made by Santa Monica Brick Company, 1924-49, is a *cuerda seca*, 6-tile mural that presents a humorous caricature of a Mexican and his horse. The cigarette and stubble add to the *caballero*'s casual demeanor as he trots through an idyllic desert setting.

Southern California's Pacific Pottery continued the high style Spanish appearance when they produced a 1930s tourist item for Valencia Oranges. The ceramic sculpture depicts two entwined dancing figures — a well-dressed *Senor* with hat and a beautiful *Senorita* in a traditional Spanish dress with a flounced skirt. The figures were mono-chromatic, made in a vivid orange.

An assortment of ceramics shows the popular "ringed" dinnerware pieces made by Bauer Company (1909-61). Located in Lincoln Heights, the company developed the ring ware in 1931 and it was copied by many other ceramic companies throughout the 1930s. The ceramic cowboy-hat ash trays were made as tourist items by Catalina Pottery (1927-37).

Wallace China, begun in 1931, produced this line of "Westward Ho" dinnerware in 1943 when M.C. Wentz commissioned it in several variations: Rodeo, Boots & Saddles and Pioneer Trails. It was heavy grade hotel china used by the popular hotels in the Western "tourist" region and was frequently bought by Californians attempting to give a Western appearance to their California ranch house.

RESOURCES

ANTIQUE MALLS

The Antique Guild
3225 & 3231 Helms Avenue, Los Angeles, California 90034-3209
Tel: 310-838-3131; Fax: 310-878-2934
www.theantiqueguild.com

Antiques on Fair Oaks
330 South Fair Oaks Avenue, Pasadena, California 91105
Tel: 626-449-9590; Fax: 626-449-9441

Cannery Row Antique Mall
471 Wave Street, Monterey, CA 93940-1424
Tel: 831 -655 0264 Fax: 831 655 0265
www.antiqnet.com/canneryrow

Great American Collective
1736 Lombard Street, San Francisco, CA 90404
Tel: 415 922 2650

Santa Monica Antique Market
1607 Lincoln Boulevard, Santa Monica, CA 90404
Tel: 310 314 4899

ANTIQUE SHOWS

Arts & Crafts, San Francisco
Concourse Exhibition Center, 8th East Brannan, San Fransico, CA 94107-2003
Tel: 707 865 1576
www.Penelope@artsandcrafts-sf.com

Bustamante Antique Shows
Tel: 209 358 3134
www.Bustamante-shows.com

The Los Angeles Pottery Show
The Pasadena Elks Lodge
Colorado Boulevard at Orange Grove, Pasadena California 91105
Tel: 909-864-1304 Fax: 909-864-1304
www.lapotteryshow.com

R.G. Canning's Rose Bowl Flea Market (2nd Sunday each month)
1 Rose Bowl Drive, Pasadena, California 91103
Tel: 323-560-7469
www.rgcshows.com

AUCTIONS

A.N. Abell Auctioneers & Appraisers
2613 Yates Avenue, Commerce, California 90040
Tel: 323-724-8102
www.abell.com

Butterfield & Butterfield Auctioneers & Appraisers
7601 West Sunset Boulevard, West Hollywood, California 90069
Tel: 323-850-7500

ARCHITECTURAL SALVAGE

Architectural Detail
512 South Fair Oaks Avenue, Pasadena, California 91105
Tel: 626-844-6670

Architectural Salvage of San Diego
1971 India Street, Suite 114, San Diego, California 92101
Tel: 619-696-1313

Tony's
123 North Olive, Orange, California 92866
Tel: 714-538-1900; Fax: 714-938-1966

FIREPLACES

Edmond's Furniture & Stone Galleries
5174 Melrose Avenue, Los Angeles, California 90038
Tel: 323-462-5787; Fax: 323 462-5894

Stone Works
8624 Melrose Avenue, West Hollywood, California 90069
Tel: 310-659-8614; Fax: 310-659-1331

ANTIQUES & ACCESSORIES

Antiques & Objects
445 South Fair Oaks Boulevard, Pasadena, California 91105
Tel: 626-796-8224; Fax: 626-796-7349

The Antique Way
11729 Santa Monica Boulevard, West Los Angeles, California 90025
Tel: 310-477-3971

Berkeley Bungalow
2508 San Pablo Avenue, Berkeley, California 94702-2013
Tel: 510-981-9520

Cobwebs
437 West Sixth Street, San Pedro, California 90731
Tel: 310-833-2008

Circa 1910
7206 Melrose Avenue, Los Angeles, California 90046
Tel: 323-965-1910

The Craftsman Home
3048 Claremont Avenue, Berkeley, California 94705-2630
Tel: 510-655-6503

Jefferson West Inc.
9310 Jefferson Boulevard, Culver City, California 90232
Tel: 310-558-3031; Fax: 310-558-4296

Mike Haskell Antiques
539 San Ysidro Road, Santa Barbara, California 93108
Tel: 805-565-1121

Life Time Gallery
7111 Melrose Avenue, Los Angeles, California 90046
Tel: 323-939-7441; Fax: 323-939-7442

Now & Then Antiques
730 Scott Court, Novato, California 94945-3226
Tel: 415-892-4436

Old California Store
1520 East Thompson Boulevard, Ventura, California 93001
Tel: 805-643-4217

Rockridge Antiques
5601 College Avenue, Oakland, California 94705
Tel: 510-652-7115

Roger Renick Fine Arts & Antiwues
696 East Colorado Boulevard, Pasadena, California 91101
Tel: 626-304-0008

Wells Antiques
2162 W. Sunset Boulevard, Los Angeles, California

Antique Reproductions

Arte de Mexico
1000 Chestnut Street, Burbank, California 91506
Tel: 818-753-4559
17092 Pullman Street, Irvine, California 92614
Tel: 949-660-1200; Fax: 949-863-0489
356 Riverton Avenue, North Hollywood, California 91601
Tel: 818-769-5090; Fax: 818-769-9425
www.arteshowrooms.com

Arroyo Craftsman
4509 Littlejohn Street, Baldwin Park, California 91706
Tel: 626-960-9411; Fax: 626-960-9521

Casa Mexicana Imports
31149 Via Coinas #609, Westlake Village, California 91362
Tel: 818-879-1974

El Paso Imports
2008 South Sepulveda Boulevard, Los Angeles, California 90025
Tel: 310-477-1936
913 State Street, Santa Barbara, California 93101
Tel: 895-963-7530
38 West Main Street, Ventura, California 93001
Tel: 805-641-2234
www.elpasoimportsco..com

Fedde's
2350 East Colorado Boulevard, Pasadena, California 91107
Tel: 626-796-7103
32 North Sierra Madre Boulevard, Pasadena, California 91107
Tel: 626-844-1160

Haven Home Furnishings
2886 Thousand Oaks Boulevard, Thousand Oaks, California 91362
Tel: 805-374-9060

Hile Studio, Inc.
1823 Enterprise Way, Monrovia, California 91016
Tel: 626-359-7210; Fax: 626-359-7320

Historic Lighting
114 East Lemon Avenue, Monrovia, California 91016
Tel: 626-303-4899; Fax: 626-358-6159
www.historiclighting.com

Rituals
756 La Cienega Boulevard, California 90069
Tel: 310-854-0848; Fax: 310-854-6126

Tile

California Art Tile
8687 Melrose Avenue, West Hollywood, California 90069
Tel: 310-659-2614

Compton Tiles
2031 Berryman Street, Berkeley, California 94709
Tel: 510-526-7356

Deer Creek Designs
305 Richardson Street, Grass Valley, California 95945
Tel: 530-477-7812

Malibu Ceramic Works
1111 North Topanga Canyon Boulevard, Topanga, California 90290
Tel: 213-455-2485; Fax: 310-455-4385

Marlo Bartels Studio
2307 Laguna Casnyon Road, Laguna, California
Tel: 949-494-4408
www.marlobartels.com

Mexican Handcrafted Tile/MC Designs
7595 Carroll Road, San Diego, California 92121
Tel: 858-689-9596; Fax 858-689-9597

Mission Tile West
853 Mission Street, South Pasadena, California 91030
Tel: 626-799-4595; Fax: 626-799-8769

Motorless Building - Building Supply Co.
2707 Fletcher Drive, Los Angeles, California
Tel: 323-663-3291
www.originalvintage-artile.com

McIntyre Tile
P. O. Box 14, Healdsburg, California 95448
Tel: 707-433-8866

Richard Keit Studio
1396 Sheffield Place, Thousand Oaks, California 91360
Tel: 804-495-5032

Walker Zanger
8750 Melrose Avenue, West Hollywood, California 90069
Tel: 310-659-1234
2980 Airway Avenue, Suite B 140, Costa Mesa, California 92626
Tel: 714-546-3571
8901 Bradley Avenue, Sun Valley, California 91352
Tel: 818-504-0235
www.walterzanger.com

Winters Tileworks
2547 8th Street, #33, Berkeley, California 94710
Tel: 510-533-7624

Metalwork

Buffalo Studio
1925 East Deere Avenue, Santa Ana, California 92705
Tel: 949-250-7333

Crown City Hardware Co.
1047 North Allen Avenue, Pasadena, California 92653

Murray's Ironworks
8632 Melrose Avenue, West Hollywood, California 90250
Tel: 310-652-0632; Fax: 310-652-0633

Textiles

Antique Textiles:
Textile Artifacts
12589 Crenshaw Boulevard, Hawthorne, California 90250
Tel: 310-676-2424; Fax: 626-676-2242
www.textileguy.com and www.archiveedition.com

Reproduction Textiles:
Arts & Crafts Period Textiles
5427 Telegraph Avenue, #W2, Oakland, California 94705
Tel: 510-654-1645; Fax: 510-654-1256
www.ACPTextile@aol.com

Online Shopping Services

www.Antiqueparlor.com

www.Circline.com
Tel: 877-411-3233

GLOSSARY

Terms are Spanish, unless otherwise indicated

Artesonado – decorative wood work

Atrio – a forecourt, entrance hall or entrance court

Azulejos – decorative tile work

Bultos – three-dimensional figures of the saints produced for the colonial Missions
and churches, ("*Santos*" were their painted counterpart)

Californio – a Spanish inhabitant of Colonial California

Campanario – wall with inset bells

Canale – channel, gutter or drain pipe

Cantina – (Mexican) a small barroom, often with open front and side walls

Churrigueresco – Spanish Baroque architectural style, circa 1650-1750, with robust
sculptural ornament

Convento – housing for a religious order

Corredor – corridor, open passageway

Cortijo – court or courtyard

Cuenca – "tub," method of decorative tile making in which colors are cleanly separated from each other in the firing process.

Cuerda Seca – "dry cord," method of decorative tile making in which colors/forms
bubble together forming a dark line between colors/forms in the firing process.

Desornamentado – reserved Spanish classical architectural style, circa 1556-1650,
inspired by Italian Renaissance works

Equipale – (Mexican) name of common and popular Mexican style furniture made of
willow and pigskin

Espadana – bell tower

Indianola – Native American community of dwellings surrounding Anglo settlements
common during early statehood across the United States

Jacal – (Mexican and Native American) adobe peasant dwellings, usually rectangular,
one room structures with thatch, palm or bark roof

Latias –(Spanish Colonial, Mex.can and Native American) stripped wood twigs laid
across roof beams of interior ceiling, and supporting roofing of thatch, palm or
tiles

Lavanderia – "laundry," Spanish colonial mission fountains used for washing

Luminaria – freestanding candle holder, usually of wrought iron

Mexicano – Mexican inhabitant of Colonial California

Mission Order Gable – phrase denoting the style of the curved arch pediment at the
entrance of Spanish missions, usually accompanied by a bell tower, flanking bell

towers or a wall with inset bells (*campanario*)

Mudéjar – (Islamic) Islamic-Arabic craft style, circa 12th to 16th centuries, influence retained in Spanish countries through 18th century

Mushrabiyah – (Islamic, also spelled *Mushrabeyeh*) window with lattice-work screen of wood which allows privacy while retaining air circulation and filtered light

Papalleria – writing desk

Plateresco – Spanish Renaissance architectural style, circa 1492-1556, influenced by decorative silverwork

Portales – hallways or corridors, usually open on one side and forming a terrace or patio to a court or courtyard

Presidio – Spanish Colonial city center with military accommodations and quarters

Ramada – Spanish term for Native American arbor structures; generally open on all sides but often added like porches to *jacal* structures

Ramona – half-Spanish, half-Native American fictional heroine of Helen Hunt Jackson's 1884 novel of the same name about the transformation of California from a colony to an American state

Reredo – ornamental screen behind an altar, or a partition

Retablo – a raised shelf, usually decorated, above an altar for a cross, lights and flowers

Ropero – chest for hanging clothes like an armoire

Saltillos – (Mexican) simple square flooring tiles

Sala – "room," the main room of a Spanish Colonial house or mission convento

Santos – "saints," painted figures of the saints and the Holy Family ("*Bultos*" were their sculptural counterpart)

Santeros – Native Americans and Mexicans who decorated Spanish Colonial missions, churches and chapels with *santos* and *bultos* images of the saints or Holy Family

Trastero – open fretwork chest originally for kitchen wares

Temescal – (Native American) cone-shaped, mud-plastered sweathouse that used dry heat from a relatively smokeless twig fire

Vargueno – multi-drawer chest with drop-leaf front, usually set on a table or chest

Vigas – (Spanish Colonial, Mexican and Native American) log roof beams, usually peeled and exposed on the interior ceiling

Yeseria – decorative stucco- or plaster-work

BIBLIOGRAPHY

Anderson, Timothy J., Eudorah M. Moore, and Robert W. Winter, editors, *California Design 1910*. Salt Lake City, Utah: California Design Publications, 1974.

Andree, Herb. *John Byers, Domestic Architecture in Southern California, 1919-1960*. Unpublished Masters thesis. Santa Barbara: University of California, 1971.

Andree, Herb, Noel Young and Patricia Halloran. *Santa Barbara Architecture, from Spanish Colonial to Modern*. Santa Barbara, California: Capra Press, 1995.

Apostol, Jane. *El Alisal, Where History Lingers*. Los Angeles: Historical Society of Southern California, 1994.

Ball, Bob. *Western Memorabilia and Collectibles*. Atglen, Pennsylvania: Schiffer Publishing Ltd., 1997.

Basten, Fred. *Beverly Hills: Portrait of a Fabled City*. Los Angeles: Douglas West Publishers, 1975.

Baum, George C. "The Spanish Mission Type." *Architectural Styles for Country Houses*, Henry H. Taylor, editor. New York: Architectural Book Publishing Co., 1919.

Baur-Heinhold, Margarete. *Wrought Iron Gratings, Gates and Railings*. Atglen, Pennsylvania: Schiffer Publishing Ltd., 1996.

Benton, Arthur B. "The California Mission and Its Influence on Pacific Coast Architecture," *Architect and Engineer*, vol. 24 (February 1911): 35-45.

Boutelle, Sara Holmes. *Julia Morgan, Architect*. New York: Abbeville Press, 1995.

Brady, Francis. *The Spanish Colonial Revival in California Architecture*. Unpublished Masters thesis. Long Beach: California State University, 1962.

Bricker, Lauren Weiss. *The Residential Architecture of Roland E. Coate*. Unpublished Masters thesis. Santa Barbara: University of California, 1982.

Burchell, Sam. "Spanish Treasures Close at Hand." *Los Angeles Times Magazine*, November 9, 1986: 28-29.

Byers, John Winford. "The Influence of Adobe in California." *California Arts and Architecture*, vol. 35 (April 1929): 29-33, 79.

Byne, Arthur and Mildred Stapley Byne. *Decorative Wooden Ceilings in Spain*. New York: G.P. Putnam's Sons, 1920.

Byne, Arthur and Mildred Stapley Byne. *Majorcan Houses and Gardens*. New York: W. Helburn, Inc., 1928.

Byne, Arthur and Mildred Stapley Byne. *Provincial Houses in Spain*. New York: W. Helburn, Inc., 1927.

Byne, Arthur and Mildred Stapley Byne. *Spanish Gardens and Patios*. Philadelphia: J.B. Lippincott, Co., 1924.

Byne, Arthur and Mildred Stapley Byne. *Spanish Interiors and Furniture*. New York: Dover Publications, 1969.

Byne, Arthur and Mildred Stapley Byne. *Spanish Ironwork*. New York: The Hispanic Society of America. 1915.

Byne, Arthur and Mildred Stapley Byne. *Spanish Art Collection of the Conde de la Almenas.* New York: American Art Association, 1927.

Carlton, Barbara Thornburgh and Lucinda Eddy. *In Harmony With the Land: Rancho Santa Fe Civic Center: Architecture of Lillian Rice.* San Diego, California: Women in Architecture and San Diego Historical Society, 1982.

Case, Walter. *History of Long Beach and Vicinity.* Chicago: Clarke Pub. Co., 1974.

Cheney, Charles. *Californian Architecture in Santa Barbara.* Santa Barbara: California Historical Society, 1929.

Cheney, Charles. *The California Planning Act of 1927.* Los Angeles: California Conference on City Planning, 1927.

Chipman, Jack. *Collector's Encyclopedia of California Pottery.* Paducah, Kentucky: Collector Books, 1995.

Clark, Alson. "Review: The California Architecture of Gordon Kaufmann." *Southern California Chapter, Society of Architectural Historians Newsletter* I, No. 3 (Summer, 1982): 3-4.

Clark, Alson. *Wallace Neff, Architect of California's Golden Age.* Santa Barbara: Capra Press, 1986.

Clark, Alson, David Gebhard, et al. *Wallace Neff, 1995-1982, The Romance of Regional Architecture.* San Marino, California: Huntington Library, 1989.

Clark, Robert Judson and Thomas S. Hines. *Los Angeles Transfer. Architecture in Southern California 1880-1980.* Los Angeles: William Andrews Clark Memorial Library, 1983.

Coate, Roland E. "The Early California House, Blending Colonial and California Forms," *California Arts and Architecture,* Vol. 35 (March 1929): 21-5.

Coffman, Taylor. *Building for Hearst and Morgan, Voices from the George Loorz Papers.* Summerland, California: Coastal Heritage Press, 1999.

Coffman, Taylor. *The Builders Behind the Castles: George Loorz & the F.C. Stolte Co.* San Luis Obispo, California: San Luis Obispo Historical Society, 1990.

Conrad, Rebecca and Chris H. Nelson. *Santa Barbara: A Guide to El Pueblo Viejo.* Santa Barbara, California: Capra Press, 1986.

Dowey, Bill. *A Brief History of Malibu and the Adamson House.* Malibu, California: California State Parks, 1995.

Finch, Christopher. "Monterey Furniture: Pieces that Recall Ranch Life and Hispanic Tradition." *Architectural Digest* (June 1976): 170-75, 204.

Fink, Augusta. *Time and the Terraced Land, History of the Palos Verdes Peninsula.* Berkeley: Howell and North Books, 1966.

Gebhard, David. "Architectural Imagery: The Missions and California." *Harvard Architectural Review* 1 (Spring 1980): 136-45.

Gebhard, David. "The Spanish Colonial Revival in Southern California." *Journal of the Society of Architectural Historians,* vol. 26 (May 1967): 131-47.

Gebhard, David. "Tile, Stucco Walls, and Arches: The Spanish Tradition in the Popular American House." *Home Sweet Home, American Domestic Vernacular Architecture.* Edited by Charles W. Moore. New York: Rizzoli International Publications, 1983.

Gebhard, David. *Santa Barbara, The Creation of a New Spain in America.* Santa

Barbara: University of California, The Art Gallery, 1982.

Gebhard, David. "Casa del Herrero, the George F. Steedman House, Montecito, California," *The Magazine Antiques,* vol. 130 (August 1986): 280-5.

Gebhard, David. "The Monterey Tradition: History Re-Ordered." *New Mexico Studies in Fine Arts* 7:14-19.

Gebhard, David. *George Washington Smith, 1876-1930, Spanish Colonial Revival in California.* Santa Barbara: University of California, The Art Gallery, 1964.

Gleye, Paul. *The Architecture of Los Angeles.* Los Angeles: Rosebud Books/Knapp Press, 1981.

Goodridch, Jean Smith. "Casa del Herrero." *Noticias, Quarterly Magazine of the Santa Barbara Historical Society,* vol. XII, no. 2 (Summer 1995): 21-43.

Hamlin, Talbot F. "What Makes it American: Architecture in the Southwest and West." *Pencil Points* 20 (December 1939): 762-76.

Hannaford, Donald, and Revel Edwards. *Spanish Colonial or Adobe Architecture of California, 1800-1850,* 1931. Stamford, Connecticut: Architectural Book Publishing Co., reprint 1990.

Henstell, Bruce. *Los Angeles: An Illustrated History.* New York: Knopf, 1980.

Heywood, Robert. *San Clemente, City of White Houses.* Laguna Niguel, California: Crown Valley Publishing, 1969.

Hitchcock, Henry-Russell. "An Eastern Critic Looks at Western Architecture." *California Arts and Architecture* 57 (December1940): 21-23, 40.

Hunter, Paul, and Walter Reichardt, editors. *Residential Architecture in Southern California.* Los Angeles: Los Angeles Chapter, American Institute of Architects, 1939.

Jackson, Helen Hunt. *Father Junipero and His Work*, 1983. El Cajon, California: Frontier Publishing Co., reprint 1966.

Jackson, Helen Hunt. *Glimpses of California and the Missions.* Boston: Little, Brown and Co., 1883.

Jackson, Helen Hunt. *Ramona,* 1884. New York: Pinnacle Book, reprint 1981.

Johnson, Reginald D. "Development of Architectural Styles in California." *Architect and Engineer* 87 (October 1926): 108-9.

Kammerling, Bruce. *Irving Gill: The Artist as Architect.* San Diego: San Diego Historical Socirty, 1979.

Kirker, Harold. *Old Forms on a New Land: California Architecture in Perspective.* Niwot, Colorado: Rhinehard Publications, 1991.

Lamb, Lucile Mead. "Adventures in Home Building." *Themis, Magazine of Zeta Tau Alpha Sorority,* November 1929. Los Angeles: Lucile Mead Lamb, reprint 1974.

Lane, Jonathan. "The Period House in the 1920's." *Journal of the Society of Architectural Historians,* vol. 20, 1961: 169-178.

Lindsey, Gaye, editor. *Tile Heritage Foundation Publications Index, 1988-1995.* Healdsburg, California: Tile Heritage Foundation, 1995.

Loe, Nancy E. *Descriptive Guide to the Julia Morgan Collection.* San Luis Obispo: California Polytechnic State University, Special Collections Department, 1985.

Lummis, Charles Fletcher. *The Home of Ramona.* Los Angeles: Charles F. Lummis

& Co., 1886.

Lmmis, Charles Fletcher. *The Spanish Pioneers.* Chicago: McClurg, A. C. & Co., 1893.

Lummis, Charles Fletcher. *The Spanish Pioneers and the California Missions.* Chicago: McClurg, A. C. & Co., 1929.

May, Cliff. *Western Ranch House.* San Francisco, California: Sunset Magazine/Lane Publishing Company, 1946.

McCoy, Esther. *Irving Gill, 1870-1936.* New York: Rheinhold Book Corp., 1958.

McMenamin, Donna. *Popular Arts of Mexico 185-1950.* Atglen, Pennsylvania: Schiffer Publishing Ltd., 1996.

McMillian, Elizabeth. *Casa California, Spanish Style Houses from Santa Barbara to San Clemente.* New York: Rizzoli International Publications, Inc., 1996.

McWilliams, Carey. *Southern California: An Island on the Land.* Salt Lake City, Utah: Peregrine Smith, Inc., 1973.

Moore, Charles, Peter Becker and Regula Campbell. *The City Observed, Los Angeles: A Guide to Its Architecture and Landscapes.* New York: Vintage Books, 1984.

Moore, Edra. "Antelope Valley Indian Museum." *Mojave Desert State Parks Visitor's Guide.* Antelope Valley: California State Parks, 1999.

Nabakov, Peter and Robert Easton. *Native American Architecture.* New York: Oxford University Press, 1989.

Neff, Wallace. *Architecture of Southern California.* Chicago: Rand McNally, 1964.

Neuerburg, Norman. *The Decoration of the California Missions.* Santa Barbara: Bellerophon Books, 1991.

Newcomb, Rexford. *The Spanish House for America.* Philadelphia: J.B. Lippincott Company, 1927.

Newcomb, Rexford. *Spanish Colonial Architecture in the United States.* New York: J.J. Augustin Publisher, 1937.

O'Gorman, Patricia W. *Tradition of Craftsmanship in Mexican Homes.* New York: Architectural Book Publishing Company, 1980.

Peixotto, Ernest. *Romantic California.* New York: Charles Scribner's Sons, 1910.

Pizzi, Donna. "Will's Wild West Showplace." *Country Sampler's West,* September/ October 1994: 28-37.

Polyzoides, Stephanos, Roger Sherwood and James Tice. *Courtyard Housing in Los Angeles, A Typological Analysis.* New York: Princeton Architectural Press, 1992.

Price, C. Mattock. "Panama-California Exposition: Bertram Goodhue and the Renaissance of Spanish Colonial Architecture." *Architectural Record* 37 (March 1915): 22-51.

Quirarte, Jacinto. *Mexican American Artists.* Austin, Texas: University of Texas Press, 1990.

Renick, Roger and Michael Trotter, editors. *Monterey Furnishings of California's Spanish Revival.* Atglen, Pennsylvania: Schiffer Publishing Ltd., 2000.

Reynolds, Jerry. *Santa Clarita: Valley of the Golden Dream.* Santa Clarita: World of Communications, 1992.

Rindge, Ronald L. and Rufus B. Keeler, *Ceramic Art of the Malibu Potteries —1926-1932.* Malibu, California: The Malibu Lagoon Museum, 1988.

Rindge, Ronald L. and Romaine S. Andaloro, Thomas W. Doyle, Tom Doyle, Charlotte H. Laubach, Judge John J. Merrick, John F. Rindge and Joseph A. Taylor. *More About Malibu Potteries — 1926-1932.* Malibu, California: The Malibu Lagoon Museum, 1997.

Rosenthal, Lee. *Catalina Tile of the Magic Isle.* Sausalito, California: Windgate Press, 1992.

Schneider, Mike. *California Potteries: The Complete Book.* Atglen, Pennsylvania: Schiffer Publishing Ltd., 1995.

Sears, M. Urmy. "The Village of Rancho Santa Fe," *California Arts and Architeture,* XXXVIII (September 1930): 36, 66.

Sexton, Randolph W. *Spanish Influence on American Architecture and Decoration.* New York: Brentano's, 1927.

Sexton, Randolph W. "A New Yorker's Impression of California Architecture." *California Arts and Architecture* 39 (October 1930): 23-24, 64.

Shorts, Don Allen. "What to Look For when Buying and Collecting Monterey Furniture" In *Monterey: An Exhibition of California Rancho Furniture, Pottery and Art.* Santa Monica, California: Santa Monica Heritage Museum: 1990.

Shorts, Don Allen. *George Mason and the Story of Monterey Furniture.* Twin Falls, Idaho: Standard Printing, 1998.

Sillo, Terry and John Manson. *Around Pasadena: An Architectural Study of San Marino, Sierra Madre and Arcadia.* Pasadena, California: Gallery Productions, 1976.

Sillo, Terry. *Excerpts from Southern California's Architectural Heritage.* Pasadena, California: Gallery Productions, 1976.

Smith, Kathryn. "Malibu Potteries." *Malibu Tile.* Los Angeles: Craft and Folk Art Museum, 1980.

Smith, Robert L. and George Mason. *Monterey: An Exhibition of California Rancho Furniture, Pottery and Art.* Santa Monica, California: Santa Monica Heritage Museum: 1990.

Snyder, Jeffrey B. *Fiesta, Homer Laughlin China Company's Colorful Dinnerware.* Atglen, Pennsylvania: Schiffer Publishing Ltd., 1997.

Soule, Winsor. *Spanish Farmhouses and Minor Public Buildings.* New York: Architectural Book Publishing Co., 1924.

Staats, H. Philip. *Californian Architecture in Santa Barbara,* 1929. Stamford, Connecticut: Architectural Book Publishing Company, Inc., reprint 1990.

Stacy-Judd, Robert B. "Some Local Examples of Mayan Adaptations." *Architect and Engineer* 116 (February 1934): 21-30.

Starr, Kevin. *Material Dreams: Southern California Through the 1920s.* New York: Oxford University Press, 1990.

Sterling, Bryan B. *The Will Rogers Scrapbook.* New York: Grosset and Dunlap, 1976.

Stern, Bill. "Color Crazed: Exposing California's Radical Pottery Past," *LA Weekly* (October 18, 1991). 14.

Stern, Bill. "Treasure Island: A Tile-By-Tile Tour of Catalina's Landmark Sites." *Westways Magazine,* vol. 24 (July 1995): 24-31.

Streatfield, David G. "The Garden at Casa del Herrero." *The Magazine Antiques,* vol. 130 (August 1986): 286-293.

Thornburg, Barbara. "Rancho Deluxe." *Los Angeles Times Magazine*, October 21, 1990: 27-37.

Tuchman, Mitch. "Bill Stern," *Magnificent Obsessions: 20 Remarkable Collectors in Pursuit of Their Dream.* San Francisco: Chronicle Books, 1994.

Weitze, Karen J. *California's Mission Revival.* Los Angeles: Hennessey & Ingalls, Inc., 1984.

Whittlesey, Austin. *The Minor Ecclesiastical, Domestic and Garden Architecture of Southern Spain.* New York: Architectural Book Publishing Co., 1917.

Witynski, Karen, and Joe P. Carr. *The New Hacienda.* Salt Lake City, Utah: Gibbs Smith, Publisher, 1999.

Zarakov, Barry Neil. *California Planned Communities of the 1920s.* Unpublished Masters thesis. Santa Barbara: University of California, 1977.

INDEX